Test-Driven Java Development

Invoke TDD principles for end-to-end application development with Java

Viktor Farcic

Alex Garcia

[PACKT] open source*
PUBLISHING   community experience distilled

BIRMINGHAM - MUMBAI

Test-Driven Java Development

First published: August 2015

Production reference: 1240815

Published by Packt Publishing Ltd.
Livery Place
35 Livery Street
Birmingham B3 2PB, UK.

ISBN 978-1-78398-742-9

www.packtpub.com

Credits

Authors
Viktor Farcic

Alex Garcia

Reviewers
Muhammad Ali

Jeff Deskins

Alvaro Garcia

Esko Luontola

Commissioning Editor
Julian Ursell

Acquisition Editor
Reshma Raman

Content Development Editor
Divij Kotian

Technical Editors
Manali Gonsalves

Naveenkumar Jain

Copy Editors
Trishya Hajare

Janbal Dharmaraj

Project Coordinator
Neha Bhatnagar

Proofreader
Safis Editing

Indexer
Priya Sane

Production Coordinator
Shantanu N. Zagade

Cover Work
Shantanu N. Zagade

About the Authors

Viktor Farcic is a software architect. He has coded using a plethora of languages, starting with Pascal (yes, he is old), Basic (before it got the Visual prefix), ASP (before it got the .Net suffix) and moving on to C, C++, Perl, Python, ASP.Net, Visual Basic, C#, JavaScript, and so on. He has never worked with Fortran. His current favorites are Scala and JavaScript, even though he works extensively on Java. While writing this book, he got sidetracked and fell in love with Polymer and GoLang.

His big passions are test-driven development (TDD), behavior-driven development (BDD), Continuous Integration, Delivery, and Deployment (CI/CD).

He often speaks at community gatherings and conferences and helps different organizations with his coaching and training sessions. He enjoys constant change and loves working with teams eager to enhance their software craftsmanship skills.

He loves sharing his experiences on his blog, `http://TechnologyConversations.com`.

I would like to thank a lot of people who have supported me during the writing of this book. The people at Everis and Defie (companies I worked with earlier) provided all the support and encouragement I needed. The technical reviewers, Alvaro Garcia, Esko Luontola, Jeff Deskins, and Muhammad Ali, did a great job by constantly challenging my views, my assumptions, and the quality of the code featured throughout the examples. Alvaro provided even more help by writing the Legacy Code chapter. His experience and expertise in the subject were an invaluable help. The Packt Publishing team was very forthcoming, professional, and always available to provide guidance and support. Finally, I'd like to give a special thanks to my daughter, Sara, and wife, Eva. With weekdays at my job and nights and weekends dedicated to this book, they had to endure months without the support and love they deserve. This book is dedicated to "my girls".

Alex Garcia started coding in C++ but later moved to Java. He is also interested in Groovy, Scala, and JavaScript. He has been working as a system administrator and also as a programmer and consultant.

He states that in the software industry, the final product quality is the key to success. He truly believes that delivering bad code always means unsatisfied customers. He is a big fan of Agile practices.

He is always interested in learning new languages, paradigms, and frameworks. When the computer is turned off, he likes to walk around sunny Barcelona and likes to practice sports.

I did enjoy writing this book and I want to thank those people who made this possible. First of all, thanks to the staff at Packt Publishing for giving me this opportunity and the guidance along this difficult journey. Thanks to the technical reviewers, Alvaro Garcia, Esko Luontola, Jeff Deskins, and Muhammad Ali, for the tips and corrections; they added great value with their comments. Thank you, Viktor Farcic, for sharing this experience with me. It has been a pleasure to be your mate during this adventure. And finally, special thanks to my parents, my brother, and my girlfriend for being there whenever I need them. This book is dedicated with love to all of them.

About the Reviewers

Muhammad Ali is a software development expert with extensive experience in telecommunications and the air and rail transport industries. He holds a master's degree in the distributed systems course of the year 2006 from the Royal Institute of technology (KTH), Stockholm, Sweden, and holds a bachelor's honors degree in computer science from the University of Engineering & Technology Lahore, Pakistan.

He has a passion for software design and development, cloud and big data test-driven development, and system integration. He has built enterprise applications using the open source stack for top-tier software vendors and large government and private organizations worldwide. Ali has settled in Stockholm, Sweden, and has been providing services to various IT companies within Sweden and outside Europe.

> I would like to thank my parents; my beloved wife; Sana Ali, and my adorable kids, Hassan and Haniya, for making my life wonderful.

Jeff Deskins has been building commercial websites since 1995. He loves to turn ideas into working solutions. Lately, he has been building most of his web applications in the cloud and is continuously learning best practices for high-performance sites.

Prior to his Internet development career, he worked for 13 years as a television news photographer. He continues to provide Internet solutions for different television stations through his website, www.tvstats.com.

> I would like to thank my wife for her support and patience through the many hours of me sitting behind my laptop learning new technologies. Love you the most!

Alvaro Garcia is a software developer who firmly believes in the eXtreme Programming methodology. He's embarked on a lifelong learning process and is now in a symbiotic exchange process with the Barcelona Software Craftsmanship meet-up, where he is a co-organizer.

Alvaro has been working in the IT industry for product companies, consulting firms, and on his own since 2005. He occasionally blogs at `http://alvarogarcia7.github.io`.

He enjoys reading and reviewing technology books and providing feedback to the author whenever possible to create the best experience for the final reader.

Esko Luontola has been programming since the beginning of the 21st century. In 2007, he was bitten by the TDD bug and has been test-infected ever since. Today, he has tens of projects under his belt using TDD and helps others get started with it; some of his freely available learning material includes the TDD Tetris Tutorial exercise and the Let's Code screencasts. He is also fluent in concurrency, distributed systems, and the deep ends of the JVM platform. In recent years, his interests have included Continuous Delivery, DevOps, and microservices.

Currently, Esko is working as a software consultant at Nitor Creations. He is the developer of multiple open source projects such as Retrolambda for back porting Java 8 code to Java 5-7 and the Jumi Test Runner in order to run tests faster and more flexibly than JUnit.

www.PacktPub.com

Support files, eBooks, discount offers, and more

For support files and downloads related to your book, please visit www.PacktPub.com.

Did you know that Packt offers eBook versions of every book published, with PDF and ePub files available? You can upgrade to the eBook version at www.PacktPub.com and as a print book customer, you are entitled to a discount on the eBook copy. Get in touch with us at service@packtpub.com for more details.

At www.PacktPub.com, you can also read a collection of free technical articles, sign up for a range of free newsletters and receive exclusive discounts and offers on Packt books and eBooks.

https://www2.packtpub.com/books/subscription/packtlib

Do you need instant solutions to your IT questions? PacktLib is Packt's online digital book library. Here, you can search, access, and read Packt's entire library of books.

Why subscribe?

- Fully searchable across every book published by Packt
- Copy and paste, print, and bookmark content
- On demand and accessible via a web browser

Free access for Packt account holders

If you have an account with Packt at www.PacktPub.com, you can use this to access PacktLib today and view 9 entirely free books. Simply use your login credentials for immediate access.

Table of Contents

Preface

Test-driven development has been around for a while and many people have still not adopted it. The reason behind this is that TDD is difficult to master. Even though the theory is very easy to grasp, it takes a lot of practice to become really proficient with it.

Authors of this book have been practicing TDD for years and will try to pass on their experience to you. They are developers and believe that the best way to learn some coding practice is through code and constant practice. This book follows the same philosophy. We'll explain all the TDD concepts through exercises. This will be a journey through the TDD best practices applied to Java development. At the end of it, you will earn a TDD black belt and have one more tool in your software craftsmanship tool belt.

What this book covers

Chapter 1, Why Should I Care for Test-driven Development?, spells out our goal of becoming a Java developer with a TDD black belt. In order to know where we're going, we'll have to discuss and find answers to some questions that will define our voyage.

Chapter 2, Tools, Frameworks, and Environments, will compare and set up all the tools, frameworks and environments that will be used throughout this book. Each of them will be accompanied with code that demonstrates their strengths and weaknesses.

Chapter 3, Red-Green-Refactor – from Failure through Success until Perfection, will help us develop a Tic-Tac-Toe game using the red-green-refactor technique, which is the pillar of TDD. We'll write a test and see it fail; we'll write a code that implements that test, run all the tests and see them succeed, and finally, we'll refactor the code and try to make it better.

Chapter 4, Unit Testing – Focusing on What You Do and Not on What Has Been Done, shows that to demonstrate the power of TDD applied to unit testing, we'll need to develop a Remote Controlled Ship. We'll learn what unit testing really is, how it differs from functional and integration tests, and how it can be combined with test-driven development.

Chapter 5, Design – If It's Not Testable, It's Not Designed Well, will help us develop a Connect4 game without any tests and try to write tests at the end. This will give us insights into the difficulties we are facing when applications are not developed in a way that they can be tested easily.

Chapter 6, Mocking – Removing External Dependencies, shows how TDD is about speed. We want to quickly demonstrate some idea/concept. We'll continue developing our Tic-Tac-Toe game by adding MongoDB as our data storage. None of our tests will actually use MongoDB since all communications to it will be mocked.

Chapter 7, BDD – Working Together with the Whole Team, discusses developing a Book Store application by using the BDD approach. We'll define the acceptance criteria in the BDD format, carry out the implementation of each feature separately, confirm that it is working correctly by running BDD scenarios, and if required, refactor the code to accomplish the desired level of quality.

Chapter 8, Refactoring Legacy Code – Making it Young Again, will help us refactor an existing application. The process will start with creation of test coverage for the existing code and from there on we'll be able to start refactoring until both the tests and the code meet our expectations.

Chapter 9, Feature Toggles – Deploying Partially Done Features to Production, will show us how to develop a Fibonacci calculator and use feature toggles to hide functionalities that are not fully finished or that, for business reasons, should not yet be available to our users.

Chapter 10, Putting It All Together, will walk you through all the TDD best practices in detail and refresh the knowledge and experience you gained throughout this book.

What you need for this book

The exercises in this book require readers to have a 64 bit computer. Installation instructions for all required software is provided throughout the book.

Who this book is for

If you're an experienced Java developer and want to implement more effective methods of programming systems and applications, then this book is for you.

Conventions

In this book, you will find a number of text styles that distinguish between different kinds of information. Here are some examples of these styles and an explanation of their meaning.

Code words in text, database table names, folder names, filenames, file extensions, pathnames, dummy URLs, user input, and Twitter handles are shown as follows: "We can include other contexts through the use of the include directive."

A block of code is set as follows:

```
public class Friendships {
    private final Map<String, List<String>> friendships = new
      HashMap<>();

    public void makeFriends(String person1, String person2) {
        addFriend(person1, person2);
        addFriend(person2, person1);
    }
```

Any command-line input or output is written as follows:

```
$> vagrant plugin install vagrant-cachier
```

```
$> git clone thttps://bitbucket.org/vfarcic/tdd-java-ch02-example-
  vagrant.git
```

New terms and **important words** are shown in bold. Words that you see on the screen, for example, in menus or dialog boxes, appear in the text like this: "Once we type our search query, we should find and click the **Go** button."

 Warnings or important notes appear in a box like this.

 Tips and tricks appear like this.

Reader feedback

Feedback from our readers is always welcome. Let us know what you think about this book—what you liked or disliked. Reader feedback is important for us as it helps us develop titles that you will really get the most out of.

To send us general feedback, simply e-mail feedback@packtpub.com, and mention the book's title in the subject of your message.

If there is a topic that you have expertise in and you are interested in either writing or contributing to a book, see our author guide at www.packtpub.com/authors.

Customer support

Now that you are the proud owner of a Packt book, we have a number of things to help you to get the most from your purchase.

Errata

Although we have taken every care to ensure the accuracy of our content, mistakes do happen. If you find a mistake in one of our books—maybe a mistake in the text or the code—we would be grateful if you could report this to us. By doing so, you can save other readers from frustration and help us improve subsequent versions of this book. If you find any errata, please report them by visiting http://www.packtpub.com/submit-errata, selecting your book, clicking on the **Errata Submission Form** link, and entering the details of your errata. Once your errata are verified, your submission will be accepted and the errata will be uploaded to our website or added to any list of existing errata under the Errata section of that title.

To view the previously submitted errata, go to https://www.packtpub.com/books/content/support and enter the name of the book in the search field. The required information will appear under the **Errata** section.

Piracy

Piracy of copyrighted material on the Internet is an ongoing problem across all media. At Packt, we take the protection of our copyright and licenses very seriously. If you come across any illegal copies of our works in any form on the Internet, please provide us with the location address or website name immediately so that we can pursue a remedy.

Please contact us at copyright@packtpub.com with a link to the suspected pirated material.

We appreciate your help in protecting our authors and our ability to bring you valuable content.

Questions

If you have a problem with any aspect of this book, you can contact us at questions@packtpub.com, and we will do our best to address the problem.

1
Why Should I Care for Test-driven Development?

This book is written by developers for developers. As such, most of the learning will be through code. Each chapter will present one or more TDD practices and we'll try to master them by solving katas. In karate, kata is an exercise where you repeat a form many times, making little improvements in each. Following the same philosophy, we'll be making small, but significant improvements from one chapter to the next. You'll learn how to design and code better, reduce time-to-market, produce always up-to-date documentation, obtain high code coverage through quality tests, and write clean code that works.

Every journey has a start and this one is no exception. Our destination is a Java developer with the **test-driven development (TDD)** black-belt.

In order to know where we're going, we'll have to discuss, and find answers, to some questions that will define our voyage. What is TDD? Is it a testing technique, or something else? What are the benefits of applying TDD?

The goal of this chapter is to obtain an overview of TDD, to understand what it is and to grasp the benefits it provides for its practitioners.

The following topics will be covered in this chapter:

- Understanding TDD
- What is TDD?
- Testing
- Mocking
- Executable documentation
- No debugging

Why TDD?

You might be working in an agile or waterfall environment. Maybe you have well-defined procedures that were battle-tested through years of hard work, or maybe you just started your own start-up. No matter what the situation was, you likely faced at least one, if not more, of the following pains, problems, or causes for unsuccessful delivery:

- Part of your team is kept out of the loop during the creation of requirements, specifications, or user stories
- Most, if not all, of your tests are manual, or you don't have tests at all
- Even though you have automated tests, they do not detect real problems
- Automated tests are written and executed when it's too late for them to provide a real value to the project
- There is always something more urgent than dedicating time to testing
- Teams are split between testing, development, and functional analysis departments, and they are often out of sync
- An inability to refactor the code because of the fear that something will be broken
- The maintenance cost is too high
- The time-to-market is too big
- Clients do not feel that what was delivered is what they asked for
- Documentation is never up to date
- You're afraid to deploy to production because the result is unknown
- You're often not able to deploy to production because regression tests take too long to run
- Team is spending too much time trying to figure out what some method or a class does

Test-driven development does not magically solve all of these problems. Instead, it puts us on the way towards the solution. There is no silver bullet, but if there is one development practice that can make a difference on so many levels, that practice is TDD.

Test-driven development speeds up the time-to-market, enables easier refactoring, helps to create better design, and fosters looser coupling.

On top of the direct benefits, TDD is a prerequisite for many other practices (continuous delivery being one of them). Better design, well-written code, faster time-to-market, up-to-date documentation, and solid test coverage, are some of the results you will accomplish by applying TDD.

It's not an easy thing to master TDD. Even after learning all the theory and going through best practices and anti-patterns, the journey is only just beginning. TDD requires time and a lot of practice. It's a long trip that does not stop with this book. As a matter a fact, it never truly ends. There are always new ways to become more proficient and faster. However, even though the cost is high, the benefits are even higher. People who spent enough time with TDD claim that there is no other way to develop a software. We are one of them and we're sure that you will be too.

We are strong believers that the best way to learn some coding technique is by coding. You won't be able to finish this book by reading it in a metro on the way to work. It's not a book that one can read in bed. You'll have to get your hands dirty and code.

In this chapter, we'll go through basics; starting from the next, you'll be learning by reading, writing, and running code. We'd like to say that by the time you're finished with this book, you'll be an experienced TDD programmer, but this is not true. By the end of this book, you'll be comfortable with TDD and you'll have a strong base in both theory and practice. The rest is up to you and the experience you'll be building by applying it in your day-to-day job.

Understanding TDD

At this time, you are probably saying to yourself "OK, I understand that TDD will give me some benefits, but what exactly is test-driven development?" TDD is a simple procedure of writing tests before the actual implementation. It's an inversion of a traditional approach where testing is performed after the code is written.

Red-green-refactor

Test-driven development is a process that relies on the repetition of a very short development cycle. It is based on the test-first concept of **extreme programming (XP)** that encourages simple design with a high level of confidence. The procedure that drives this cycle is called **red-green-refactor**.

The procedure itself is simple and it consists of a few steps that are repeated over and over again:

1. Write a test.
2. Run all tests.
3. Write the implementation code.
4. Run all tests.
5. Refactor.
6. Run all tests.

Since a test is written before the actual implementation, it is supposed to fail. If it doesn't, the test is wrong. It describes something that already exists or it was written incorrectly. Being in the green state while writing tests is a sign of a false positive. Tests like these should be removed or refactored.

[While writing tests, we are in the red state. When the implementation of a test is finished, all tests should pass and then we will be in the green state.]

If the last test failed, implementation is wrong and should be corrected. Either the test we just finished is incorrect or the implementation of that test did not meet the specification we had set. If any but the last test failed, we broke something and changes should be reverted.

When this happens, the natural reaction is to spend as much time as needed to fix the code so that all tests are passing. However, this is wrong. If a fix is not done in a matter of minutes, the best thing to do is to revert the changes. After all, everything worked not long ago. Implementation that broke something is obviously wrong, so why not go back to where we started and think again about the correct way to implement the test? That way, we wasted minutes on a wrong implementation instead of wasting much more time to correct something that was not done right in the first place. Existing test coverage (excluding the implementation of the last test) should be sacred. We change the existing code through intentional refactoring, not as a way to fix recently written code.

[Do not make the implementation of the last test final, but provide just enough code for this test to pass.]

Write the code in any way you want, but do it fast. Once everything is green, we have confidence that there is a safety net in the form of tests. From this moment on, we can proceed to refactor the code. This means that we are making the code better and more optimum without introducing new features. While refactoring is in place, all tests should be passing all the time.

If, while refactoring, one of the tests failed, refactor broke an existing functionality and, as before, changes should be reverted. Not only that at this stage we are not changing any features, but we are also not introducing any new tests. All we're doing is making the code better while continuously running all tests to make sure that nothing got broken. At the same time, we're proving code correctness and cutting down on future maintenance costs.

Once refactoring is finished, the process is repeated. It's an endless loop of a very short cycle.

Speed is the key

Imagine a game of ping pong (or table tennis). The game is very fast; sometimes it is hard to even follow the ball when professionals play the game. TDD is very similar. TDD veterans tend not to spend more than a minute on either side of the table (test and implementation). Write a short test and run all tests (ping), write the implementation and run all tests (pong), write another test (ping), write implementation of that test (pong), refactor and confirm that all tests are passing (score), and then repeat—ping, pong, ping, pong, ping, pong, score, serve again. Do not try to make the perfect code. Instead, try to keep the ball rolling until you think that the time is right to score (refactor).

Time between switching from tests to implementation (and vice versa) should be measured in minutes (if not seconds).

It's not about testing

T in TDD is often misunderstood. Test-driven development is the way we approach the design. It is the way to force us to think about the implementation and to what the code needs to do before writing it. It is the way to focus on requirements and implementation of just one thing at a time—organize your thoughts and better structure the code. This does not mean that tests resulting from TDD are useless—it is far from that. They are very useful and they allow us to develop with great speed without being afraid that something will be broken. This is especially true when refactoring takes place. Being able to reorganize the code while having the confidence that no functionality is broken is a huge boost to the quality.

The main objective of test-driven development is testable code design with tests as a very useful side product.

Testing

Even though the main objective of test-driven development is the approach to code design, tests are still a very important aspect of TDD and we should have a clear understanding of two major groups of techniques as follows:

- Black-box testing
- White-box testing

The black-box testing

Black-box testing (also known as functional testing) treats software under test as a black-box without knowing its internals. Tests use software interfaces and try to ensure that they work as expected. As long as functionality of interfaces remains unchanged, tests should pass even if internals are changed. Tester is aware of what the program should do, but does not have the knowledge of how it does it. Black-box testing is most commonly used type of testing in traditional organizations that have testers as a separate department, especially when they are not proficient in coding and have difficulties understanding it. This technique provides an external perspective on the software under test.

Some of the advantages of black-box testing are as follows:

- Efficient for large segments of code
- Code access, understanding the code, and ability to code are not required
- Separation between user's and developer's perspectives

Some of the disadvantages of black-box testing are as follows:

- Limited coverage, since only a fraction of test scenarios is performed
- Inefficient testing due to tester's lack of knowledge about software internals
- Blind coverage, since tester has limited knowledge about the application

If tests are driving the development, they are often done in the form of acceptance criteria that is later used as a definition of what should be developed.

Automated black-box testing relies on some form of automation such as **behavior-driven development** (BDD).

The white-box testing

White-box testing (also known as clear-box testing, glass-box testing, transparent-box testing, and structural testing) looks inside the software that is being tested and uses that knowledge as part of the testing process. If, for example, an exception should be thrown under certain conditions, a test might want to reproduce those conditions. White-box testing requires internal knowledge of the system and programming skills. It provides an internal perspective on the software under test.

Some of the advantages of white-box testing are as follows:

- Efficient in finding errors and problems
- Required knowledge of internals of the software under test is beneficial for thorough testing
- Allows finding hidden errors
- Programmers introspection
- Helps optimizing the code
- Due to the required internal knowledge of the software, maximum coverage is obtained

Some of the disadvantages of white-box testing are as follows:

- It might not find unimplemented or missing features
- Requires high-level knowledge of internals of the software under test
- Requires code access
- Tests are often tightly coupled to the implementation details of the production code, causing unwanted test failures when the code is refactored.

White-box testing is almost always automated and, in most cases, has the form of unit tests.

 When white-box testing is done before the implementation, it takes the form of **TDD**.

The difference between quality checking and quality assurance

The approach to testing can also be distinguished by looking at the objectives they are trying to accomplish. Those objectives are often split between **quality checking (QC)** and **quality assurance (QA)**. While quality checking is focused on defects identification, quality assurance tries to prevent them. QC is product-oriented and intends to make sure that results are as expected. On the other hand, QA is more focused on processes that assure that quality is built-in. It tries to make sure that correct things are done in the correct way.

While quality checking had a more important role in the past, with the emergence of TDD, **acceptance test-driven development (ATDD)**, and later on **behavior-driven development (BDD)**, focus has been shifting towards quality assurance.

Better tests

No matter whether one is using black-box, white-box, or both types of testing, the order in which they are written is very important.

Requirements (specifications and user stories) are written before the code that implements them. They come first so they define the code, not the other way around. The same can be said for tests. If they are written after the code is done, in a certain way, that code (and the functionalities it implements) is defining tests. Tests that are defined by an already existing application are biased. They have a tendency to confirm what code does, and not to test whether client's expectations are met, or that the code is behaving as expected. With manual testing, that is less the case since it is often done by a siloed QC department (even though it's often called QA). They tend to work on tests' definition in isolation from developers. That in itself leads to bigger problems caused by inevitably poor communication and the *police syndrome* where testers are not trying to help the team to write applications with quality built-in, but to find faults at the end of the process. The sooner we find problems, the cheaper it is to fix them.

 Tests written in the TDD fashion (including its flavors such as ATDD and BDD) are an attempt to develop applications with quality built-in from the very start. It's an attempt to avoid having problems in the first place.

Mocking

In order for tests to run fast and provide constant feedback, code needs to be organized in such a way that the methods, functions, and classes can be easily replaced with mocks and stubs. A common word for this type of *replacements* of the actual code is test double. Speed of the execution can be severely affected with external dependencies; for example, our code might need to communicate with the database. By mocking external dependencies, we are able to increase that speed drastically. Whole unit tests suite execution should be measured in minutes, if not seconds. Designing the code in a way that it can be easily mocked and stubbed, forces us to better structure that code by applying separation of concerns.

More important than speed is the benefit of removal of external factors. Setting up databases, web servers, external APIs, and other dependencies that our code might need, is both time consuming and unreliable. In many cases, those dependencies might not even be available. For example, we might need to create a code that communicates with a database and have someone else create a schema. Without mocks, we would need to wait until that schema is set.

 With or without mocks, the code should be written in a way that we can easily replace one dependency with another.

Executable documentation

Another very useful aspect of TDD (and well-structured tests in general) is documentation. In most cases, it is much easier to find out what the code does by looking at tests than the implementation itself. What is the purpose of some methods? Look at the tests associated with it. What is the desired functionality of some part of the application UI? Look at the tests associated with it. Documentation written in the form of tests is one of the pillars of TDD and deserves further explanation.

The main problem with (traditional) software documentation is that it is not up to date most of the time. As soon as some part of the code changes, the documentation stops reflecting the actual situation. This statement applies to almost any type of documentation, with requirements and test cases being the most affected.

The necessity to document code is often a sign that the code itself is not well written. Moreover, no matter how hard we try, documentation inevitably gets outdated.

Developers shouldn't rely on system documentation because it is almost never up to date. Besides, no documentation can provide as detailed and up-to-date description of the code as the code itself.

Using code as documentation, does not exclude other types of documents. The key is to avoid duplication. If details of the system can be obtained by reading the code, other types of documentation can provide quick guidelines and a high-level overview. Non-code documentation should answer questions such as what the general purpose of the system is and what technologies are used by the system. In many cases, a simple **README** is enough to provide the quick start that developers need. Sections such as project description, environment setup, installation, and build and packaging instructions are very helpful for newcomers. From there on, code is the bible.

Implementation code provides all needed details while test code acts as the description of the intent behind the production code.

 Tests are executable documentation with TDD being the most common way to create and maintain it.

Assuming that some form of **Continuous Integration** (**CI**) is in use, if some part of test-documentation is incorrect, it will fail and be fixed soon afterwards. CI solves the problem of incorrect test-documentation, but it does not ensure that all functionality is documented. For this reason (among many others), test-documentation should be created in the TDD fashion. If all functionality is defined as tests before the implementation code is written and execution of all tests is successful, then tests act as a complete and up-to-date information that can be used by developers.

What should we do with the rest of the team? Testers, customers, managers, and other non coders might not be able to obtain the necessary information from the production and test code.

As we saw earlier, two most common types of testing are black-box and white-box testing. This division is important since it also divides testers into those who do know how to write or at least read code (white-box testing) and those who don't (black-box testing). In some cases, testers can do both types. However, more often than not, they do not know how to code so the documentation that is usable for developers is not usable for them. If documentation needs to be decoupled from the code, unit tests are not a good match. That is one of the reasons why BDD came in to being.

 BDD can provide documentation necessary for non-coders, while still maintaining the advantages of TDD and automation.

Customers need to be able to define new functionality of the system, as well as to be able to get information about all the important aspects of the current system. That documentation should not be too technical (code is not an option), but it still must be always up to date. BDD narratives and scenarios are one of the best ways to provide this type of documentation. Ability to act as **acceptance criteria** (written before the code), be executed frequently (preferably on every commit), and be written in natural language makes BDD stories not only always up to date, but usable by those who do not want to inspect the code.

Documentation is an integral part of the software. As with any other part of the code, it needs to be tested often so that we're sure that it is accurate and up to date.

 The only cost-effective way to have accurate and up-to-date information is to have executable documentation that can be integrated into your continuous integration system.

TDD as a methodology is a good way to move towards this direction. On a low level, unit tests are a best fit. On the other hand, BDD provides a good way to work on a functional level while maintaining understanding accomplished using natural language.

No debugging

We (authors of this book) almost never debug applications we're working on!

This statement might sound pompous, but it's true. We almost never debug because there is rarely a reason to debug an application. When tests are written before the code and the code coverage is high, we can have high confidence that the application works as expected. This does not mean that applications written using TDD do not have bugs—they do. All applications do. However, when that happens, it is easy to isolate them by simply looking for the code that is not covered with tests.

Tests themselves might not include some cases. In that situation, the action is to write additional tests.

 With high code coverage, finding the cause of some bug is much faster through tests than spending time debugging line by line until the culprit is found.

Summary

In this chapter, you got the general understanding of test-driven development practice and insights into what TDD is and what it isn't. You learned that it is a way to design the code through short and repeatable cycle called red-green-refactor. Failure is an expected state that should not only be embraced, but enforced throughout the TDD process. This cycle is so short that we move from one phase to another with great speed.

While code design is the main objective, tests created throughout the TDD process are a valuable asset that should be utilized and severely impact on our view of traditional testing practices. We went through the most common of those practices such as white-box and black-box testing, tried to put them into the TDD perspective, and showed benefits that they can bring to each other.

You discovered that mocks are a very important tool that is often a must when writing tests. Finally, we discussed how tests can and should be utilized as executable documentation and how TDD can make debugging much less necessary.

Now that we are armed with theoretical knowledge, it is time to set up the development environment and get an overview and comparison of different testing frameworks and tools.

2
Tools, Frameworks, and Environments

"We become what we behold. We shape our tools and then our tools shape us."

Marshall McLuhan

As every soldier knows his weapons, a programmer must be familiar with the development ecosystem and those tools that make programming much easier. Whether you are already using any of these tools at work or home, it is worth taking a look at many of them and comparing the features, advantages, and disadvantages. Let's do an overview of what we can find nowadays about the following topics and construct a small project to get familiar with some of them.

We won't go into the details of those tools and frameworks since that will be done later on in the following chapters. The goal is to get you up and running and provide you with a short overview of what they do and how.

The following topics will be covered in this chapter:

- Git
- Virtual machines
- Build tools
- The integrated development environment
- Unit testing frameworks
- Code coverage tools
- Mocking frameworks
- User interface testing
- Behavior-driven development

Git

Git is the most popular revision control system. For that reason, all the code used in this book is stored in Bitbucket (`https://bitbucket.org/`). If you don't have it already, install Git. Distributions for all the popular operating systems can be found at `http://git-scm.com`.

Many graphical interfaces are available for Git; some of them being Tortoise (`https://code.google.com/p/tortoisegit`), Source Tree (`https://www.sourcetreeapp.com`), and Tower (`http://www.git-tower.com/`).

Virtual machines

Even though they are outside the topic of this book, virtual machines are a powerful tool and a first-class citizen in a good development environment. They provide dynamic and easy-to-use resources in isolated systems so they can be used and dropped at the time we need them. This helps developers to focus on their tasks instead of wasting their time creating or installing required services from scratch. This is the reason why virtual machines have found room in here. We want to take advantage of them to keep you focused on the code.

In order to have the same environment no matter the OS you're using, we'll be creating virtual machines with Vagrant and deploying required applications with Docker. We chose Ubuntu as a base operating system in our examples, just because it is a popular, commonly used Unix-like distribution. Most of these technologies are platform-independent, but occasionally you won't be able to follow the instructions found here because you might be using some other operating system. In that case, your task is to find what the differences are between Ubuntu and your operating system and act accordingly.

Vagrant

Vagrant is the tool we are going to use for creating the development environment stack. It is an easy way to initialize ready-to-go virtual machines with minimum effort using preconfigured boxes. All boxes and configurations are placed in one file, called **Vagrant file**.

Here is an example of creating a simple Ubuntu box. We made an extra configuration for installing MongoDB using Docker (the usage of Docker will be explained shortly). We assume that you have VirtualBox (`https://www.virtualbox.org`) and Vagrant (`https://www.vagrantup.com`) installed on your computer and that you have Internet access.

In this particular case, we are creating an instance of Ubuntu 64-bits using the Ubuntu box (`ubuntu/trusty64`) and specifying that the VM should have 1 GB of RAM:

```
config.vm.box = "ubuntu/trusty64"

config.vm.provider "virtualbox" do |vb|
vb.memory = "1024"
end
```

Further on, we're exposing MongoDB's default port in the Vagrant machine and running it using Docker:

```
config.vm.network "forwarded_port", guest: 27017, host: 27017
config.vm.provision "docker" do |d|
  d.run "mongoDB", image: "mongo:2", args: "-p 27017:27017"
end
```

Finally, in order to speed up the Vagrant setup, we're caching some resources. You should install the plugin called **cachier**. For further information, visit `https://github.com/fgrehm/vagrant-cachier`.

```
if Vagrant.has_plugin?("vagrant-cachier")
  config.cache.scope = :box
end
```

Now it's time to see it working. It usually takes a few minutes to run it for the first time because the base box and all the dependencies need to be downloaded and installed:

```
$> vagrant plugin install vagrant-cachier
$> git clone thttps://bitbucket.org/vfarcic/tdd-java-ch02-example-vagrant.git
$> cd tdd-java-ch02-example-vagrant
$> vagrant up
```

When this command is run, you should see the following output:

```
vfarcic@viktor:~/IdeaProjects/tdd-java-ch02-example-vagrant$ vagrant up
Bringing machine 'default' up with 'virtualbox' provider...
==> default: Importing base box 'ubuntu/trusty64'...
==> default: Matching MAC address for NAT networking...
==> default: Checking if box 'ubuntu/trusty64' is up to date...

==> default: Setting the name of the VM: tdd-java-ch02-example-vagrant_default_1435347519969_47040
==> default: Clearing any previously set forwarded ports...
==> default: Clearing any previously set network interfaces...
==> default: Preparing network interfaces based on configuration...
    default: Adapter 1: nat
==> default: Forwarding ports...
    default: 27017 => 27017 (adapter 1)
    default: 22 => 2222 (adapter 1)
==> default: Running 'pre-boot' VM customizations...
==> default: Booting VM...
==> default: Waiting for machine to boot. This may take a few minutes...
    default: SSH address: 127.0.0.1:2222
    default: SSH username: vagrant
    default: SSH auth method: private key
    default: Warning: Connection timeout. Retrying...
    default:
    default: Vagrant insecure key detected. Vagrant will automatically replace
    default: this with a newly generated keypair for better security.
    default:
    default: Inserting generated public key within guest...
    default: Removing insecure key from the guest if its present...
    default: Key inserted! Disconnecting and reconnecting using new SSH key...
==> default: Machine booted and ready!
==> default: Checking for guest additions in VM...
==> default: Mounting shared folders...
    default: /vagrant => /home/vfarcic/IdeaProjects/tdd-java-ch02-example-vagrant
    default: /tmp/vagrant-cache => /home/vfarcic/.vagrant.d/cache/ubuntu/trusty64
==> default: Configuring cache buckets...
==> default: Running provisioner: docker...
    default: Installing Docker (latest) onto machine...
    default: Configuring Docker to autostart containers...
==> default: Starting Docker containers...
==> default: -- Container: mongoDB
==> default: Configuring cache buckets...
vfarcic@viktor:~/IdeaProjects/tdd-java-ch02-example-vagrant$ █
```

Be patient until the execution is finished. Once done, you'll have a new virtual machine with Ubuntu. Docker and one MongoDB instance up and running. The best part is that all this was accomplished with a single command.

To see the status of the currently running VM, we can use the status argument:

```
$> vagrant status

Current machine states:

default                      running (virtualbox)
```

Virtual machine can be accessed either through SSH or by using Vagrant commands as in the following example:

```
$> vagrant ssh
Welcome to Ubuntu 14.04.2 LTS (GNU/Linux 3.13.0-46-generic x86_64)

 * Documentation:  https://help.ubuntu.com/

 System information disabled due to load higher than 1.0

  Get cloud support with Ubuntu Advantage Cloud Guest:
    http://www.ubuntu.com/business/services/cloud

0 packages can be updated.
0 updates are security updates.


vagrant@vagrant-ubuntu-trusty-64:~$
```

Finally, to stop the virtual machine, exit from it and run the `vagrant halt` command:

```
$> exit
$> vagrant halt
==> default: Attempting graceful shutdown of VM...
$>
```

 For the list of Vagrant boxes or further details about configuring Vagrant, visit https://www.vagrantup.com.

Docker

Once the environment is set, it is time to install the services and the software that we need. This can be done using Docker, a simple and portable way to ship and run many applications and services in isolated containers. We will use it to install the required databases, web servers, and all the other applications required throughout this book, in a virtual machine created using Vagrant. In fact, the Vagrant VM that was previously created already has an example of getting up and running an instance of MongoDB using Docker.

Let's bring up the VM again (we stopped it previously with the `vagrant halt` command) and also MongoDB:

```
$> vagrant up
$> vagrant ssh
 vagrant@vagrant-ubuntu-trusty-64:~$ docker start mongoDB
 vagrant@vagrant-ubuntu-trusty-64:~$ docker ps
CONTAINER ID        IMAGE           COMMAND             CREATED
360f5340d5fc        mongo:2         "/entrypoint.sh mong   41 minutes ago

STATUS              PORTS                       NAMES
Up 41 minutes       0.0.0.0:27017->27017/tcp    mongoDB
vagrant@vagrant-ubuntu-trusty-64:~$ exit
```

With `docker start`, we started the container; with `docker ps`, we listed all the running processes.

By using this kind of procedure, we are able to reproduce a full-stack environment in the blink of an eye. You may be wondering if this is as awesome as it sounds. The answer is yes, it is. Vagrant and Docker allow developers to focus on what they are supposed to do and forget about complex installations and tricky configurations. Furthermore, we made an extra effort to provide you with all necessary steps and resources to reproduce and test all the code examples and demonstrations in this book.

Build tools

With time, code tends to grow both in complexity and size. This occurs in the software industry by its nature. All products evolve constantly and new requirements are made and implemented across a product's life. Build tools offer a way to make managing project life cycle's as straightforward as possible, by following a few code conventions such as the organization of your code in a specific way and usage of naming a convention for your classes or a determined project structure formed by different folders and files.

Some of you might be familiar with Maven or Ant. They are a great couple of Swiss army knives for handling projects, but we are here to learn so we decided to use Gradle. Some of the advantages of Gradle are reduced boiler plate code, resulting in a much `shortdr` file and a more readable `configuration` file. Among others, Google uses it as its build tool. It is supported by IntelliJ IDEA and is quite easy to learn and work with. Most of the functionalities and tasks are obtained by adding plugins.

Mastering Gradle is not the goal of this book. So, if you want to learn more about this awesome tool, take a tour through its web page (`http://gradle.org/`) and read about the plugins you can use and the options you can customize. For a comparison of different Java build tools, visit `http://technologyconversations.com/2014/06/18/build-tools/` or `http://technologyconversations.com/2014/06/18/build-tools/`.

Before proceeding forward, make sure that Gradle is installed on your system.

Let's analyze the relevant parts of a `build.gradle` file. It holds project information in a concise way using Groovy as the descriptor language. This is our project's build file, autogenerated with IntelliJ:

```
apply plugin: 'java'
sourceCompatibility = 1.7
version = '1.0'
```

A Java plugin is applied since it is a Java project. It brings common Java tasks such as build, package, test, and so on. The source compatibility is set to JDK 7. The compiler will complain if we try to use the Java syntax that is not supported by this version:

```
repositories {
    mavenCentral()
}
```

Maven Central (`http://search.maven.org/`) holds all our project dependencies. This section tells Gradle where to pull them from. The Maven Central repository is enough for this project, but you can add your custom repositories, if any. Nexus and ivy are also supported:

```
dependencies {
    testCompile group: 'junit', name: 'junit', version: '4.12'
}
```

Last, but not least, this is how project dependencies are declared. IntelliJ decided to use JUnit as the testing framework.

Gradle tasks are easy to run. For example, to run tests from the command prompt, we can simply execute the following:

`gradle test`

This can be accomplished from IDEA by running the test task from the Gradle Tool Window that can be accessed from **View** | **Tool Windows** | **Gradle**.

The tests result is stored in the HTML files that are located in the **build | reports | tests** directory.

The following is the test report generated by running `gradle test` against the sample code:

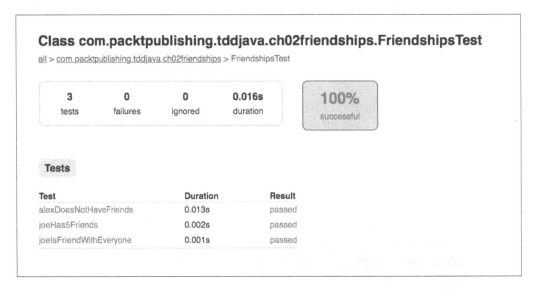

The integrated development environment

As many tools and technologies will be covered, we recommend using IntelliJ IDEA as the tool for code development. The main reason is that this IDE works without any tedious configuration. The **Community Edition (IntelliJ IDEA CE)** comes with a bunch of built-in features and plugins that make coding easy and efficient. It automatically recommends plugins that can be installed depending on the file extension. As IntelliJ IDEA is the choice we made for this book, you will find references and steps referring to its actions or menus. Readers should find a proper way to emulate those steps if they are using other IDEs. Refer to `https://www.jetbrains.com/idea/` for instructions on how to download and install IntelliJ IDEA.

The IDEA demo project

Let's create the base layout of the demo project. This project will be throughout along this chapter to illustrate all the topics that are covered. Java will be the programming language and Gradle (`http://gradle.org/`) will be used to run different sets of tasks such as building, testing, and so on.

Let us import into IDEA the repository that contains examples from this chapter:

1. Open IntelliJ IDEA, select **Check out from Version Control,** and click on **Git.**

2. Type `https://bitbucket.org/vfarcic/tdd-java-ch02-example-junit.git` in the Git repository URL and click on **Clone. Confirm** for the rest of the IDEA questions until a new project is created with code cloned from the Git repository.

The imported project should look similar to the following image:

Now that we have got the project set up, it's time to take a look at unit testing frameworks.

Unit testing frameworks

In this section, two of the most used Java frameworks for unit testing are shown and briefly commented on. We will focus on their syntax and main features by comparing a test class written using both **JUnit** and **TestNG**. Although there are slight differences, both frameworks offer the most commonly-used functionalities, and the main difference is how tests are executed and organized.

Let's start with a question. What is a test? How can we define it?

A test is a repeatable process or method that verifies the correct behavior of a tested target in a determined situation with a determined input expecting a predefined output or interactions.

In the programming approach, there are several types of tests depending on their scope: functional tests, acceptance tests, and unit tests. Further on, we will explore each of those types of tests in more detail.

Unit testing is about testing small pieces of code. Let's see how to test a single Java class. The class is quite simple, but enough for our interest:

```java
public class Friendships {
    private final Map<String, List<String>> friendships =
      new HashMap<>();

    public void makeFriends(String person1, String person2) {
        addFriend(person1, person2);
        addFriend(person2, person1);
    }

    public List<String> getFriendsList(String person) {
        if (!friendships.containsKey(person)) {
            return Collections.emptyList();
        }
        return friendships.get(person);
    }

    public boolean areFriends(String person1, String person2) {
        return friendships.containsKey(person1) &&
        friendships.get(person1).contains(person2);
    }
}
```

```
    private void addFriend(String person, String friend) {
        if (!friendships.containsKey(person)) {
            friendships.put(person, new ArrayList<String>());
        }
        List<String> friends = friendships.get(person);
        if (!friends.contains(friend)) {
            friends.add(friend);
        }
    }
}
```

JUnit

JUnit (http://junit.org/) is a simple and easy-to-learn framework for writing and running tests. Each test is mapped as a method, and each method should represent a specific known scenario in which a part of our code will be executed. The code verification is made by comparing the expected output or behavior with the actual output.

The following is the test class written with JUnit. There are some scenarios missing, but for now we are interested in showing what tests look like. We will focus on better ways to test our code and on best practices later in this book.

Tests classes usually consist of three stages; set up, tests and tear down. Let's start with methods that set up data needed for tests. A setup can be performed on a class or method level:

```
Friendships friendships;

@BeforeClass
public static void beforeClass() {
    // This method will be executed once on initialization time
}

@Before
public void before() {
    friendships = new Friendships();
    friendships.makeFriends("Joe", "Audrey");
    friendships.makeFriends("Joe", "Peter");
    friendships.makeFriends("Joe", "Michael");
    friendships.makeFriends("Joe", "Britney");
    friendships.makeFriends("Joe", "Paul");
}
```

The `@BeforeClass` annotation specifies a method that will be run once before any of the test methods in the class. It is a useful way to do some general setup that will be used by most (if not all) tests.

The `@Before` annotation specifies a method that will be run before each test method. We can use it to set up test data without worrying that the tests that are run afterwards will change the state of that data. In the example above, we're instantiating the `Friendships` class and adding five sample entries to the `Frienships` list. No matter what changes will be performed by each individual test, this data will be recreated over and over until all the tests are performed.

Common examples of usage of those two annotations is setting up of database data, creation of files needed for tests, and so on. Later on, we'll see how external dependencies can and should be avoided using mocks. Nevertheless, functional or integration tests might still need those dependencies and the `@Before` and `@BeforeClass` annotations are a good way to set them up.

Once data is set up, we can proceed with the actual tests:

```java
@Test
public void alexDoesNotHaveFriends() {
  Assert.assertTrue("Alex does not have friends",
    friendships.getFriendsList("Alex").isEmpty());
}

@Test
public void joeHas5Friends() {
  Assert.assertEquals("Joe has 5 friends", 5,
    friendships.getFriendsList("Joe").size());
}

@Test
public void joeIsFriendWithEveryone() {
  List<String> friendsOfJoe =
  Arrays.asList("Audrey", "Peter", "Michael", "Britney", "Paul");
Assert.assertTrue(friendships.getFriendsList("Joe")
.containsAll(friendsOfJoe));
}
```

In this example, we are using a few of the many different types of asserts. We're confirming that Alex does not have any friends, while Joe is a very popular guy with five friends (Audrey, Peter, Michael, Britney, and Paul).

Finally, once the tests are finished, we might need to perform some clean up:

```
@AfterClass
public static void afterClass() {
    // This method will be executed once when all test are executed
}

@After
public void after() {
    // This method will be executed once after each test execution
}
```

In our example, in the `Friendships` class, we have no need to clean up anything. If there were such a need, those two annotations would provide that feature. They work in a similar fashion to the `@Before` and `@BeforeClass` annotations. `@AfterClass` is run once all tests are finished. The `@After` annotation is executed after each test. This runs each `test` method as a separate class instance. As long as we are avoiding global variables and external resources such as databases and APIs, each test is isolated from the others. Whatever was done in one, does not affect the rest.

The complete source code can be found in the `FriendshipsTest` class in the `https://github.com/TechnologyConversations/tdd-java-ch02-example-junit.git` or `https://bitbucket.org/vfarcic/tdd-java-ch02-example-junit.git` repositories.

TestNG

In TestNG (`http://testng.org/doc/index.html`), tests are organized in classes, just as in the case of JUnit.

The following Gradle configuration (`build.gradle`) is required in order to run TestNG tests:

```
dependencies {
    testCompile group: 'org.testng', name: 'testng', version: '6.8.21'
}

test.useTestNG(){
// Optionally you can filter which tests are executed using
//     exclude/include filters
//excludeGroups 'complex'
}
```

Unlike JUnit, TestNG requires additional Gradle configuration that tells it to use TestNG to run tests.

The following test class is written with TestNG and is a reflection of what we did earlier with JUnit. Repeated imports and other boring parts are omitted with the intention of focusing on the relevant parts:

```
@BeforeClass
public static void beforeClass() {
    // This method will be executed once on initialization time
}

@BeforeMethod
public void before() {
    friendships = new Friendships();
    friendships.makeFriends("Joe", "Audrey");
    friendships.makeFriends("Joe", "Peter");
    friendships.makeFriends("Joe", "Michael");
    friendships.makeFriends("Joe", "Britney");
    friendships.makeFriends("Joe", "Paul");
}
```

You probably already noticed the similarities between JUnit and TestNG. Both are using annotations to specify what the purposes of certain methods are. Besides different names (@Beforeclass vs @BeforeMethod), there is no difference between the two. However, unlike Junit, TestNG reuses the same test class instance for all test methods. This means that the test methods are not isolated by default, so more care is needed in the before and after methods.

Asserts are very similar as well:

```
public void alexDoesNotHaveFriends() {
  Assert.assertTrue(friendships.getFriendsList("Alex").isEmpty(),
  "Alex does not have friends");
}
public void joeHas5Friends() {
  Asert.assertEquals(friendships.getFriendsList("Joe").size(),
    5, "Joe has 5 friends");
}
public void joeIsFriendWithEveryone() {
  List<String> friendsOfJoe =
  Arrays.asList("Audrey", "Peter", "Michael", "Britney", "Paul");
  Assert.assertTrue(friendships.getFriendsList("Joe")
  .containsAll(friendsOfJoe));
}
```

The only notable difference when compared with Junit is the order of the `assert` variables. While JUnit assert's order of arguments is optional message, expected values, and actual values, TestNG's order is actual value, expected value and optional message. Besides the difference in the order of arguments we're passing to the `assert` methods, there are almost no differences between JUnit and TestNG.

You might have noticed that `@Test` is missing. TestNG allows us to set it on the class level and thus convert all public methods into tests.

The `@After` annotations are also very similar. The only notable difference is the TestNG `@AfterMethod` annotations that acts in the same way as the JUnit `@After` annotation.

As you can see, the syntax is pretty similar. Tests are organized in to classes and test verifications are made using assertions. That is not to say that there are no more important differences between those two frameworks; we'll see some of them throughout this book. I invite you to explore JUnit (`http://junit.org/`) and TestNG (`http://testng.org/`) by yourself.

The complete source code with the examples above can be found at `https://bitbucket.org/vfarcic/tdd-java-ch02-example-testng.git`.

The assertions we have written until now are using only the testing frameworks. However, there are some test utilities that can help us make them nicer and more readable.

Hamcrest and AssertJ

In the previous section, we gave an overview of what a unit test is and how it can be written using two of the most commonly used Java frameworks. Since tests are an important part of our projects, why not improve the way we write them? Some cool projects emerged, aiming to empower the semantic of tests by changing the way assertions are made. As a result, tests are more concise and easier to understand.

Hamcrest

Hamcrest adds a lot of methods called matchers. Each matcher is designed to perform a comparison operation. It is extensible enough to support custom matchers created by yourself. Furthermore, JUnit supports Hamcrest natively since its core is included in the JUnit distribution. You can start using Hamcrest effortlessly. However, we want to use the full-featured project so we will add a test dependency to Gradle's file:

```
testCompile 'org.hamcrest:hamcrest-all:1.3'
```

Let us compare one assert from JUnit with the equivalent one from Hamcrest:

- **The JUnit assert**:

```
List<String> friendsOfJoe =
Arrays.asList("Audrey", "Peter", "Michael", "Britney", "Paul");
    Assert.assertTrue( friendships.getFriendsList ("Joe")
    .containsAll(friendsOfJoe)
    );
```

- **The Hamcrest assert**:

```
assertThat(
        friendships.getFriendsList("Joe"),
        containsInAnyOrder("Audrey", "Peter",
         "Michael", "Britney", "Paul")
    );
```

As you can see, Hamcrest is a bit more expressive. It has a much bigger range of asserts that allows us to avoid some boilerplate code and, at the same time, makes code easier to read and has more expressive code.

Here's another example:

- **JUnit assert**:

```
Assert.assertEquals(5, friendships.getFriendsList("Joe").size());
```

- **Hamcrest assert**:

```
assertThat(friendships.getFriendsList("Joe"), hasSize(5));
```

You'll notice two differences. The first is that, unlike JUnit, Hamcrest works almost always with direct objects. While in the case of JUnit, we needed to get the integer size and compare it with the expected number (5); Hamcrest has a bigger range of asserts so we can simply use one of them (`hasSize`) together with the actual object (`List`). Another difference is that Hamcrest has the inverse order with actual value being the first argument (like TestNG).

Those two examples are not enough to show the full potential offered by Hamcrest. Later on in this book, there will be more examples and explanations of Hamcrest. Visit https://code.google.com/p/hamcrest/ or http://hamcrest.org/ and explore its syntax.

The complete source code can be found in the `FriendshipsHamcrestTest` class in the https://github.com/TechnologyConversations/tdd-java-ch02-example-junit.git or https://bitbucket.org/vfarcic/tdd-java-ch02-example-junit.git repositories.

AssertJ

AssertJ works in a similar way to Hamcrest. A major difference is that AssertJ assertions can be concatenated.

To work with AssertJ, the dependency must be added to Gradle's dependencies:

```
testCompile 'org.assertj:assertj-core:2.0.0'
```

Let's compare JUnit asserts with AssertJ:

```
Assert.assertEquals(5, friendships.getFriendsList("Joe").size());
List<String> friendsOfJoe =
  Arrays.asList("Audrey", "Peter", "Michael", "Britney", "Paul");
Assert.assertTrue(  friendships.getFriendsList("Joe")
  .containsAll (friendsOfJoe)
);
```

The same two asserts can be concatenated to a single one in AssertJ:

```
assertThat(friendships.getFriendsList("Joe"))
        .hasSize(5)
        .containsOnly("Audrey", "Peter", "Michael", "Britney",
            "Paul");
```

This was a nice improvement. There was no need to have two separate asserts, nor there was a need to create a new list with expected values. Moreover, AssertJ is more readable and easier to understand.

The complete source code can be found in the `FriendshipsAssertJTest` class in the `https://github.com/TechnologyConversations/tdd-java-ch02-example-junit.git` or `https://bitbucket.org/vfarcic/tdd-java-ch02-example-junit.git` repositories.

Now that we have tests up and running, we might want to see what is the code coverage is generated with our tests.

Code coverage tools

The fact that we wrote tests does not mean that they are good, nor that they cover enough code. As soon as we start writing and running tests, the natural reaction is to start asking questions that were not available before. What parts of our code are properly tested? What are the cases that our tests did not take into account? Are we testing enough? These and other similar questions can be answered with code coverage tools. They can be used to identify the blocks or lines of code that were not covered by our tests; they can also calculate the percentage of code covered and provide other interesting metrics.

They are powerful tools used to obtain metrics and show relations between tests and implementation code. However, as with any other tool, their purpose needs to be clear. They do not provide information about quality, but only about which parts of our code have been tested.

 Code coverage shows whether the code lines are reached during test execution, but it is not a guarantee of good testing practices because test quality is not included on these metrics.

Let's take a look at one of the most popular tools used to calculate code coverage.

JaCoCo

Java Code Coverage (JaCoCo) is a well-known tool for measuring test coverage. To use it in our project, we need to add a few lines to our Gradle configuration file, that is, `build.gradle`:

1. Add the Gradle plugin for JaCoCo:

    ```
    apply plugin: 'jacoco'
    ```

2. To see the JaCoCo results, run the following from your command prompt:

    ```
    gradle test jacocoTestReport
    ```

3. The same Gradle tasks can be run from the **Gradle Tasks IDEA Tool Window**.

4. The end result is stored in the **build | reports | jacoco | test | html** directory. It's an HTML file that can be opened in any browser:

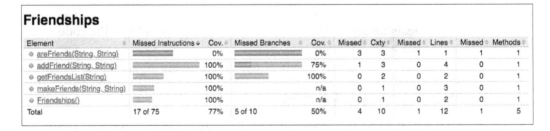

Friendships

Element	Missed Instructions	Cov.	Missed Branches	Cov.	Missed	Cxty	Missed	Lines	Missed	Methods
areFriends(String, String)		0%		0%	3	3	1	1	1	1
addFriend(String, String)		100%		75%	1	3	0	4	0	1
getFriendsList(String)		100%		100%	0	2	0	2	0	1
makeFriends(String, String)		100%		n/a	0	1	0	3	0	1
Friendships()		100%		n/a	0	1	0	2	0	1
Total	17 of 75	77%	5 of 10	50%	4	10	1	12	1	5

Further chapters of this book will explore Code Coverage in more detail. Until then, go to `http://www.eclemma.org/jacoco/` for more information.

Mocking frameworks

Our project looks cool, but it's too simple and it is far from being a real project. It still doesn't use external resources. A database is required by Java projects so we'll try to introduce it, as well.

What is the common way to test code that uses external resources or third-party libraries? Mocks are the answer. A mock object, or simply a mock, is a simulated object that can be used to replace real ones. They are very useful when objects that depend on external resources are deprived of them.

In fact, you don't need a database at all while you are developing the application. Instead, you can use mocks to speed up development and testing and use a *real* database connection only at runtime. Instead of spending time setting up a database and preparing test data, we can focus on writing classes and think about them later on during integration time.

For demonstration purposes, we'll introduce two new classes. The `Person` class and the `FriendCollection` class that are designed to represent persons and database object mapping. Persistence will be done with MongoDB (`https://www.mongodb.org/`).

Our sample will have two classes. `Person` will represent database object data; `FriendCollection` will be our data access layer. The code is, hopefully, self-explanatory.

Let's create and use the `Person` class:

```
public class Person {
    @Id
    private String name;

    private List<String> friends;

    public Person() { }

    public Person(String name) {
        this.name = name;
        friends = new ArrayList<>();
    }

    public List<String> getFriends() {
        return friends;
    }
```

```java
        public void addFriend(String friend) {
            if (!friends.contains(friend)) friends.add(friend);
        }

    }
```

Let's create and use the `FriendsCollection` class:

```java
    public class FriendsCollection {
        private MongoCollection friends;

        public FriendsCollection() {
            try {
                DB db = new MongoClient().getDB("friendships");
                friends = new Jongo(db).getCollection("friends");
            } catch (UnknownHostException e) {
                throw new RuntimeException(e.getMessage());
            }
        }

        public Person findByName(String name) {
            return friends.findOne("{_id: #}", name).as(Person.class);
        }

        public void save(Person p) {
            friends.save(p);
        }
    }
```

In addition, some new dependencies have been introduced so the Gradle dependencies block needs to be modified, as well. The first one is the **MongoDB** driver, which is required to connect to the database. The second is **Jongo**, a small project that makes accessing Mongo collections pretty straightforward.

The Gradle dependencies for `mongodb` and `jongo` are as follows:

```
    dependencies {
        compile 'org.mongodb:mongo-java-driver:2.13.2'
        compile 'org.jongo:jongo:1.1'
    }
```

We are using a database so the `Friendships` class should also be modified. We should change a map to `FriendsCollection` and modify the rest of the code to use it. The end result is the following:

```
public class FriendshipsMongo {
    private FriendsCollection friends;

    public FriendshipsMongo() {
        friends = new FriendsCollection();
    }

    public List<String> getFriendsList(String person) {
        Person p = friends.findByName(person);
        if (p == null)   return Collections.emptyList();
        return p.getFriends();
    }

    public void makeFriends(String person1, String person2) {
        addFriend(person1, person2);
        addFriend(person2, person1);
    }

    public boolean areFriends(String person1, String person2) {
        Person p = friends.findByName(person1);
        return p != null && p.getFriends().contains(person2);
    }

    private void addFriend(String person, String friend) {
        Person p = friends.findByName(person);
        if (p == null)   p = new Person(person);
        p.addFriend(friend);
        friends.save(p);
    }
}
```

The complete source code can be found in the `FriendsCollection` and `FriendshipsMongo` classes in the `https://bitbucket.org/vfarcic/tdd-java-ch02-example-junit.git` repository.

Now that we have our `Friendships` class working with MongoDB, let's take a look at one possible way to test it by using mocks.

Mockito

Mockito is a Java framework that allows easy creation of the test double.

The Gradle dependency is the following:

```
dependencies {
    testCompile group: 'org.mockito', name: 'mockito-all', version: '1.+'
}
```

Mockito runs through the JUnit runner. It creates all the required mocks for us and injects them into the class with tests. There are two basic approaches; instantiating mocks by ourselves and injecting them as class dependencies via a class constructor or using a set of annotations. In the next example, we are going to see how is it done using annotations.

In order for a class to use Mockito annotations, it needs to be run with `MockitoJUnitRunner`. Using the runner simplifies the process because you just simply add annotations to objects to be created:

```
@RunWith(MockitoJUnitRunner.class)
public class FriendshipsTest {
...
}
```

In your test class, the tested class should be annotated with `@InjectMocks`. This tells Mockito which class to inject mocks into:

```
@InjectMocks
FriendshipsMongo friendships;
```

From then on, we can specify which specific methods or objects inside the class, in this case `FriendshipsMongo`, will be substituted with mocks:

```
@Mock
FriendsCollection friends;
```

In this example, `FriendsCollection` inside the `FriendshipsMongo` class will be mocked.

Now, we can specify what should be returned when `friends` is invoked:

```
Person joe = new Person("Joe");
doReturn(joe).when(friends).findByName("Joe");
assertThat(friends.findByName("Joe")).isEqualTo(joe);
```

In this example, we're telling Mockito to return the `joe` object whenever `friends.findByName("joe")` is invoked. Later on, we're verifying with `assertThat` that this assumption is correct.

Let's try to do the same test as we did previously in the class that was without MongoDB:

```
@Test
public void joeHas5Friends() {
    List<String> expected =
Arrays.asList("Audrey", "Peter", "Michael", "Britney", "Paul");
    Person joe = spy(new Person("Joe"));

    doReturn(joe).when(friends).findByName("Joe");
    doReturn(expected).when(joe).getFriends();

    assertThat(friendships.getFriendsList("Joe"))
        .hasSize(5)
    .containsOnly("Audrey", "Peter", "Michael", "Britney", "Paul");
}
```

A lot of things happened in this small test. First, we're specifying that `joe` is a spy. In Mockito, spies are real objects that use real methods unless specified otherwise. Then, we're telling Mockito to return `joe` when the `friends` method calls `getFriends`. This combination allows us to return the `expected` list when the `getFriends` method is invoked. Finally, we're asserting that the `getFriendsList` returns the expected list of names.

The complete source code can be found in the `FriendshipsMongoAssertJTest` class in the `https://bitbucket.org/vfarcic/tdd-java-ch02-example-junit.git` repository.

We'll use Mockito later on; throughout this book, you'll get your chance to become more familiar with it and mocking in general. More information about Mockito can be found at `http://mockito.org/`.

EasyMock

EasyMock is an alternative mocking framework. It is very similar to Mockito. However, the main difference is that EasyMock does not create spy objects but mocks. Other differences are syntactical.

Let's see an example of EasyMock. We'll use the same set of test cases as those that were used for Mockito examples:

```
@RunWith(EasyMockRunner.class)
public class FriendshipsTest {
    @TestSubject
    FriendshipsMongo friendships = new FriendshipsMongo();
    @Mock(type = MockType.NICE)
    FriendsCollection friends;
```

Essentially, the runner does the same as the Mockito runner:

```
@TestSubject
FriendshipsMongo friendships = new FriendshipsMongo();

@Mock(type = MockType.NICE)
FriendsCollection friends;
```

The `@TestSubject` annotation is similar to Mockito's `@InjectMocks`, while the `@Mock` annotation denotes an object to be mocked in a similar fashion to Mockito's `@Mock`. Furthermore, the type `nice` tells the mock to return empty.

Let's compare one of the asserts we did with Mockito:

```
@Test
public void mockingWorksAsExpected() {
    Person joe = new Person("Joe");
    expect(friends.findByName("Joe")).andReturn(joe);
    replay(friends);
    assertThat(friends.findByName("Joe")).isEqualTo(joe);
}
```

Besides small differences in syntax, the only disadvantage of EasyMock is that the additional instruction `replay` was needed. It tells the framework that the previously specified expectation should be applied. The rest is almost the same. We're specifying that `friends.findByName` should return the `joe` object, applying that expectation and, finally, asserting whether the actual result is as expected.

In the EasyMock version, the second `test` method that we used with Mockito is the following:

```
@Test
public void joeHas5Friends() {
    List<String> expected =
    Arrays.asList("Audrey", "Peter", "Michael", "Britney", "Paul");
    Person joe = createMock(Person.class);
```

```
expect(friends.findByName("Joe")).andReturn(joe);
expect(joe.getFriends()).andReturn(expected);
replay(friends);
replay(joe);

assertThat(friendships.getFriendsList("Joe"))
        .hasSize(5)
        .containsOnly("Audrey", "Peter", "Michael", "Britney",
         "Paul");
}
```

Again, there are almost no differences when compared to Mockito, except that EasyMock does not have spies. Depending on the context, that might be an important difference.

Even though both frameworks are similar, there are small details that makes us choose Mockito as a framework, which will be used throughout this book.

 Visit `http://easymock.org/` for more information about this asserts library.

The complete source code can be found in the `FriendshipsMongoEasyMockTest` class in the `https://bitbucket.org/vfarcic/tdd-java-ch02-example-junit.git` or `https://github.com/TechnologyConversations/tdd-java-ch02-example-junit.git` repositories.

Extra power for mocks

Both projects introduced above do not cover all types of methods or fields. Depending on the applied modifiers such static or final, a class, method, or field can be out of range for Mockito or EasyMock. In such as cases, we can use PowerMock to extend the mocking framework. This way, we can mock objects that can only be mocked in a tricky manner. However, one should be cautious with PowerMock since the necessity to use many of the features it provides is usually a sign of poor design. If you're working on a legacy code, PowerMock might be a good choice. Otherwise, try to design your code in a way that PowerMock is not needed. We'll show you how to do that later on.

For more information, visit `https://code.google.com/p/powermock/`.

User interface testing

Even though unit testing can and should cover the major part of the application, there is still a need to work on functional and acceptance tests. Unlike unit tests, they provide higher-level verifications, and are usually performed at entry points, and rely heavily on user interface. At the end, we are creating applications that are, in most cases, used by humans, so being confident of our application's behavior is very important. This comfort status can be achieved by testing what the application is expected to do, from the point of view of real users.

Here, we'll try to provide an overview of functional and acceptance testing through a user interface. We'll use the Web as an example, even though there are many other types of user interfaces such as desktop applications, smart phone interfaces, and so on.

Web testing frameworks

The `application` classes and data sources have been tested throughout this chapter, but there is still something missing; the most common user entry point – the Web. Most enterprise applications such as intranets or corporate sites are accessed using the browser. For this reason, testing Web provides a significant value, helping us to make sure that it is doing what it is expected to do.

Furthermore, companies are investing a lot of time performing long and heavy manual tests every time the application changes. This is a big waste of time since a lot of those tests can be automatized and executed without supervision, using tools such as **Selenium** or **Selenide**.

Selenium

Selenium is a great tool for Web testing. It uses a browser to run verifications and it can handle all the popular browsers such as Firefox, Safari, and Chrome. It also supports headless browsers to test web pages with much greater speed and less resources consumption.

There is a `SeleniumIDE` plugin that can be used to create tests by recording actions performed by the user. Currently, it is only supported by Firefox. Sadly, even though tests generated this way provide very fast results, they tend to be very brittle and cause problems in the long run, especially when some part of a page changes. For this reason, we'll stick with the code written without the help from that plugin.

The simplest way to execute Selenium is to run it through `JUnitRunner`. All Selenium tests start by initializing `WebDriver`, the class used for communication with browsers:

1. Let's start by adding the Gradle dependency:

   ```
   dependencies {
     testCompile 'org.seleniumhq.selenium:selenium- java:2.45.0'
   }
   ```

2. As an example, we'll create a test that searches Wikipedia. We'll use a Firefox driver as our browser of choice:

   ```
   WebDriver driver = new FirefoxDriver();
   ```

WebDriver is an interface that can be instantiated with one of the many drivers provided by Selenium:

1. To open an URL, the instruction would be following:

   ```
   driver.get
       ("http://en.wikipedia.org/wiki/Main_Page");
   ```

2. Once the page is opened, we can search for an input element by its name and then type some text:

   ```
   WebElement query =
   driver.findElement(By.name("search"));
   query.sendKeys("Test-driven development");
   ```

3. Once we type our search query, we should find and click the **Go** button:

   ```
   WebElement goButton =
   driver.findElement(By.name("go"));
   goButton.click();
   ```

4. Once we reach our destination, it is time to validate that, in this case, the page title is correct:

   ```
   assertThat(driver.getTitle(),
   startsWith("Test-driven development"));
   ```

5. Finally, the driver should be closed once we're finished using it:

   ```
   driver.quit();
   ```

That's it. We have a small but valuable test that verifies a single use case. While there is much more to be said about Selenium, hopefully, this has provided you with enough information to realize the potential behind it.

Visit `http://www.seleniumhq.org/` for further information and more complex use of WebDriver.

The complete source code can be found in the `SeleniumTest` class in the `https://bitbucket.org/vfarcic/tdd-java-ch02-example-web.git` repository.

While Selenium is the most commonly used framework to work with browsers, it is still very low level and requires a lot of tweaking. Selenide was born out of the idea that Selenium would be much more useful if there wasa higher level library that could implement some of the common patterns and solve the often repeated needs.

Selenide

What we have seen about Selenium is very cool. It brings the opportunity to probe that our application is doing things well, but sometimes it is a bit tricky to configure and use. Selenide is a project based on Selenium that offers a good syntax for writing tests and makes them more readable. It hides the usage of WebDriver and configurations from you, while still maintaining a high level of customization:

1. Like all the other libraries we have used until now, the first step is to add the Gradle dependency:

```
dependencies {
    testCompile 'com.codeborne:selenide:2.17'
}
```

2. Let's see how we can write the previous Selenium test using Selenide instead. The syntax might be familiar to for those who know JQuery (`https://jquery.com/`):

```
public class SelenideTest {
    @Test
    public void wikipediaSearchFeature() throws
      InterruptedException {
        // Opening Wikipedia page
        open("http://en.wikipedia.org/wiki/Main_Page");

        // Searching TDD
        $(By.name("search")).setValue("Test-driven" +
          " development");

        // Clicking search button
        $(By.name("go")).click();
```

```
        // Checks
        assertThat(title(), startsWith("Test-driven" +
          " development"));
    }
}
```

This was a more expressive way to write a test. On top of a more fluent syntax, there are some things that happen behind this code and would require additional lines of Selenium. For example, a click action will wait until an element in question is available, and will fail only if the predefined period of time expired. Selenium, on the other hand, would fail immediately. In today's world, with many elements being loaded dynamically through JavaScript, we cannot expect everything to appear at once. Hence, this Selenide feature proves to be useful and saves us from repetitive boilerplate code. There are many other benefits Selenide brings to the table. Due to the benefits that Selenide provides when compared with Selenium, it will be our framework of choice throughout this book. Furthermore, there is a whole chapter dedicated to Web testing using this framework. Visit `http://selenide.org/` for more information on ways to use Web drivers in your tests.

No matter whether tests were written with one framework or the another, the effect is the same. When tests are run, a Firefox browser window will emerge and execute all steps defined in the test sequentially. Unless a headless browser was chosen as your driver of choice, you will be able to see what is going on throughout the test. If something goes wrong, a failure trace is available. On top of that, we can take browser screenshots at any point. For example, it is a common practice to record the situation at the time of a failure.

The complete source code can be found in the `SelenideTest` class in the `https://bitbucket.org/vfarcic/tdd-java-ch02-example-web.git` repository.

Armed with a basic knowledge of Web testing frameworks, it is time to take a short look at BDD.

The behavior-driven development

Behavior-driven development (BDD) is an agile process designed to keep the focus on a stakeholder value throughout the whole project. The premise of BDD is that the requirement has to be written in a way that everyone—be they business representative, analyst, developer, tester, manager, and so on—understands it. The key is to have a unique set of artefacts that are understood and used by everyone—a collection of user stories. Stories are written by the whole team and used as both requirements and executable test cases. It is a way to perform TDD with a clarity that cannot be accomplished with unit testing. It is a way to describe and test functionality in (almost) natural language and make it runnable and repeatable.

A story is composed of scenarios. Each scenario represents a concise behavioral use case and is written in natural language using steps. Steps are a sequence of the preconditions, events, and outcomes of a scenario. Each step must start with the words Given, When, or Then. Given is for preconditions, When is for actions, and Then is for performing validations.

This was only a brief introduction. There is a whole chapter, *Chapter 7, BDD - Working Together with the Whole Team*, dedicated to this topic. Now, it is time to introduce JBehave and Cucumber as two of the many available frameworks for writing and executing stories.

JBehave

JBehave is a Java BDD framework used for writing acceptance tests that are able to be executed and automated. The steps used in stories are bound to Java code through several annotations provided by the framework:

1. First of all, add JBehave to Gradle dependencies:

```
dependencies {
    ...
        testCompile 'org.jbehave:jbehave-core:3.9.5'
    ...
}
```

2. Let's go through a few example steps:

```
@Given("I go to Wikipedia homepage")
public void goToWikiPage() {
    open("http://en.wikipedia.org/wiki/Main_Page");
}
```

3. This is the given type of step. It represents a precondition that needs to be fulfilled for some actions to be performed successfully. In this particular case, it will open a Wikipedia page. Now that we have our precondition specified, it is time to define some actions:

```
@When("I enter the value $value on a field named " +
  "$fieldName")
public void enterValueOnFieldByName(String value,
  String fieldName){
    $(By.name(fieldName)).setValue(value);
}
@When("I click the button $buttonName")
public void clickButtonByName(String buttonName){
    $(By.name(buttonName)).click();
}
```

4. As you can see, actions are defined with the When annotation. In our case, we can use those steps to set some value to a field or click on a specific button. Once actions are performed, we can deal with validations. Note that steps can be more flexible by introducing parameters:

```
@Then("the page title contains $title")
public void pageTitleIs(String title) {
    assertThat(title(), containsString(title));
}
```

Validations are declared using the Then annotation. In this example, we are validating the page title as expected.

These steps can be found in the WebSteps class in the https://bitbucket.org/vfarcic/tdd-java-ch02-example-web.git repository.

Once we have defined our steps, it is time to use them. The following story combines those steps in order to validate a desired behavior:

```
Scenario: TDD search on wikipedia
```

It starts with naming the scenario. The name should be as concise as possible, but enough to identify the user case unequivocally; it is for informative purposes only:

```
Given I go to Wikipedia homepage
When I enter the value Test-driven development on a field named search
When I click the button go
Then the page title contains Test-driven development
```

As you can see, we are using the same steps text that we defined earlier. The code related to those steps will be executed in a sequential order. If any of them, the execution is halted and the scenario itself is considered failed.

Even though we defined our steps ahead of stories, it can be done the other way around with a story being defined first and the steps following. In that case, the status of a scenario would be pending, meaning that the required steps are missing.

This story can be found in the wikipediaSearch.story file in the https://bitbucket.org/vfarcic/tdd-java-ch02-example-web.git repository.

To run this story, execute the following:

```
$> gradle testJBehave
```

While the story is running, we can see that actions are taking place in the browser. Once it is finished, a report with the results of an execution is generated. It can be found in `build/reports/jbehave`.

---

bdd/jbehave/stories/wikipediaSearch.story

Scenario: Wikipedia search

Given I go to Wikipedia homepage
When I enter the value Test-driven development on a field named search
When I click the button go
Then the page title contains Test-driven development

JBehave story execution report

For brevity, we excluded the `build.gradle` code to run JBehave stories. The completed source code can be found in the `https://bitbucket.org/vfarcic/tdd-java-ch02-example-web.git` repository.

 For further information on JBehave and its benefits, visit `http://jbehave.org/`.

Cucumber

Cucumber was originally a Ruby BDD framework. These days it supports several languages including Java. It provides functionality that is very similar to JBehave.

Let's see the same examples written in Cucumber.

The same as any other dependency we have used until now, Cucumber needs to be added to `build.gradle` before we can start using it:

```
dependencies {
    ...
    testCompile 'info.cukes:cucumber-java:1.2.2'
    testCompile 'info.cukes:cucumber-junit:1.2.2'
    ...
}
```

We will create the same steps as we did with JBehave, using the Cucumber way:

```
@Given("^I go to Wikipedia homepage$")
public void goToWikiPage() {
    open("http://en.wikipedia.org/wiki/Main_Page");
}

@When("^I enter the value (.*) on a field named (.*)$")
public void enterValueOnFieldByName(String value,
    String fieldName){
    $(By.name(fieldName)).setValue(value);
}

@When("^I click the button (.*)$")
public void clickButonByName(String buttonName){
    $(By.name(buttonName)).click();
}

@Then("^the page title contains (.*)$")
public void pageTitleIs(String title) {
    assertThat(title(), containsString(title));
}
```

The only noticeable difference between these two frameworks is the way Cucumber defines steps text. It uses regular expressions to match variables types, unlike JBehave that deduces them from a method signature.

The steps code can be found in the `WebSteps` class in the `https://bitbucket.org/ vfarcic/tdd-java-ch02-example-web.git` repository:

Let's see how the story looks when written using the Cucumber syntax:

```
Feature: Wikipedia Search

  Scenario: TDD search on wikipedia
    Given I go to Wikipedia homepage
    When I enter the value Test-driven development on a field named search
    When I click the button go
    Then the page title contains Test-driven development
```

Note that there are almost no differences. This story can be found in the `wikipediaSearch.feature` file in the `https://bitbucket.org/vfarcic/tdd-java-ch02-example-web.git` repository.

As you might have guessed, to run a Cucumber story, all you need to do is run the following Gradle task:

```
$> gradle testCucumber
```

The result reports are located in the `build/reports/cucumber-report` directory. This is the report for the above story.

▼ **Feature**: Wikipedia Search
    ▼ **Scenario**: TDD search on wikipedia
        Given I go to Wikipedia homepage
        When I enter the value Test-driven development on a field named search
        When I click the button go
        Then the page title contains Test-driven development

Cucumber story execution report

The full code example can be found in the `https://bitbucket.org/vfarcic/tdd-java-ch02-example-web.git` repository.

 For a list of languages supported by Cucumber or for any other details, visit `https://cukes.info/`.

Since both JBehave and Cucumber offer a similar set of features, we decided to use JBehave throughout the rest of this book. There is a whole chapter dedicated to BDD and JBehave.

Summary

In this chapter, we took a break from TDD and introduced many tools and frameworks that will be used for code demonstrations in the rest of the chapters. We set up everything from version control, virtual machines, building tools, and IDE, until we reached frameworks that are commonly used as today's testing tools.

We are big proponents of the open source movement. Following this spirit, we made a special effort to select free tools and frameworks in every category.

Now that we have set up all the tools that we will need, it is time to go deeper into TDD, starting with the red-green-refactor procedure—TDD's cornerstone.

3
Red-Green-Refactor – from Failure through Success until Perfection

"Knowing is not enough; we must apply. Willing is not enough; we must do."

- Bruce Lee

The **red-green-refactor** technique is the basis of TDD. It is a game of ping pong in which we are switching between tests and implementation code at great speed. We'll fail, then we'll succeed and, finally, we'll improve.

We'll develop a Tic-Tac-Toe game by going through each requirement one at a time. We'll write a test and see if it fails. Then, we'll write a code that implements that test, run all the tests, and see them succeed. Finally, we'll refactor the code and try to make it better. This process will be repeated many times until all the requirements are successfully implemented.

We'll start by setting up the environment with Gradle and JUnit. Then, we'll go a bit deeper into the red-green-refactor process. Once we're ready with the setup and theory, we'll go through the high-level requirements of the application.

With everything set, we'll dive right into the code—one requirement at a time. Once everything is done, we'll take a look at the code coverage and decide whether it is acceptable or more tests need to be added.

The following topics will be covered in this chapter:

- Setting up the environment with Gradle and JUnit
- The red-green-refactor process
- Tic-Tac-Toe requirements
- Developing Tic-Tac-Toe
- Code coverage
- More exercises

Setting up the environment with Gradle and JUnit

You are probably familiar with the setup of Java projects. However, you might not have worked with IntelliJ IDEA before or you might have used Maven instead of Gradle. In order to make sure that you can follow the exercise, we'll quickly go through the setup.

Setting up Gradle/Java project in IntelliJ IDEA

The main purpose of this book is to teach TDD, so we will not go into detail about Gradle and IntelliJ IDEA. Both are used as an example. All exercises in this book can be done with different choices for IDE and build tools. You can, for example, use Maven and Eclipse instead. For most, it might be easier to follow the same guidelines as those presented throughout the book, but the choice is yours.

The following steps will create a new `Gradle` project in IntelliJ IDEA:

1. Open **IntelliJ IDEA**. Click on **Create New Project** and select **Gradle** from the left-hand side menu. Then, click on **Next**.

2. If you are using IDEA 14 and higher, you will be asked for an **Artifact ID**. Type **tdd-java-ch03-tic-tac-toe** and click on **Next** twice. Type **tdd-java-ch03-tic-tac-toe** as the project name. Then, click on the **Finish** button.

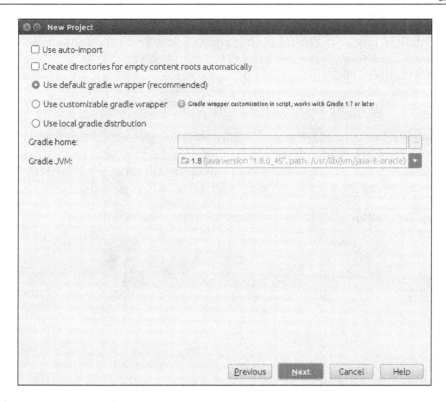

In the **New Project** dialog, we can observe that IDEA has already created the `build.
gradle` file. Open it and you'll see that it already contains the **JUnit** dependency.
Since this is our framework of choice in this chapter, there is no additional
configuration that we should do. By default, `build.gradle` is set to use Java 1.5
as a source compatibility setting. You can change it to any version you prefer. The
examples in this chapter will not use any of the Java features that came after version
5, but that doesn't mean that you cannot solve the exercise using, for example, JDK 8.

Our `build.gradle` file should look like the following:

```
apply plugin: 'java'

version = '1.0'

repositories {
    mavenCentral()`
}

dependencies {
    testCompile group: 'junit', name: 'junit',
        version: '4.11'
}
```

Now, all that's left is to create packages that we'll use for tests and the implementation. From the **Project** dialog, right click to bring the **context** menu and select **New | Directory**. Type `src/test/java/com/packtpublishing/tddjava/` `ch03tictactoe` and click on the **OK** button to create the `tests` package. Repeat the same steps with the `src/main/java/com/packtpublishing/tddjava/` `ch03tictactoe` directory to create the implementation package.

Finally, we need to the make test and implementation classes. Create the `TicTacToeSpec` class inside the `com.packtpublishing.tddjava.ch03tictactoe` package in the `src/test/java` directory. This class will contain all our tests. Repeat the same for the `TicTacToe` class in the `src/main/java` directory.

Your **Project** structure should be similar to the one presented in the screenshot below:

The source code can be found in the `00-setup` branch of the `tdd-java-ch03-` `tic-tac-toe` Git repository at `https://bitbucket.org/vfarcic/tdd-java-ch03-` `tic-tac-toe/branch/00-setup`.

Always separate tests from the implementation code.

The benefits are as follows: this avoids accidentally packaging tests together with production binaries; many build tools expect tests to be in a certain source directory.

A common practice is to have at least two source directories. The implementation code should be located in `src/main/java` and the test code in `src/test/java`. In bigger projects, the number of source directories can increase, but the separation between implementation and tests should remain.

Build tools such as Maven and Gradle expect source directories' separation, as well as naming conventions.

That's it. We're set to start working on our *Tic-Tac-Toe* application using JUnit as the testing framework of choice and Gradle for compilation, dependencies, testing, and other tasks. In *Chapter 1, Why Should I Care for Test-driven Development?*, you first encountered the red-green-refactor procedure. Since it is the cornerstone of TDD and is the main objective of the exercise in this chapter, it might be a good idea to go into a bit more detail before we start the development.

The red-green-refactor process

The red-green-refactor process is the most important part of TDD. It is the main pillar, without which no other aspect of TDD will work.

The name comes from the states our code is within the cycle. When in red state, code does not work; when in the green state, everything is working as expected, but not necessarily in the best possible way. Refactor is the phase when we know that features are well covered with tests and thus gives us the confidence to change it and make it better.

Write a test

Every new feature starts with a test. The main objective of this test is to focus on requirements and code design before writing the code. A test is a form of an executable documentation and can be used later on to get an understanding of what the code does or what are the intentions behind it.

At this point, we are in the red state since the execution of tests fails. There is a discrepancy between what tests expect from the code and what the implementation code actually does. To be more specific, there is no code that fulfils the expectation of the last test; we did not write it yet. It is possible that at this stage all the tests are actually passing, but that's the sign of a problem.

Run all the tests and confirm that the last one is failing

Confirming that the last test is failing, confirms that the test would not, mistakenly, pass without the introduction of a new code. If the test is passing, then the feature already exists or the test is producing a false positive. If that's the case and the test actually always passes independently of implementation, it is, in itself, worthless and should be removed.

A test must not only fail, but must fail for the expected reason.

In this phase, we are still in the *red* stage. Tests were run and the last one failed.

Write the implementation code

The purpose of this phase is to write code that will make the last test pass. Do not try to make it perfect, nor try to spend too much time with it. If it's not well written or is not optimum, that is still okay. It'll become better later on. What we're really trying to do is to create a safety net in the form of tests that are confirmed to pass. Do not try to introduce any functionality that was not described in the last test. To do that, we are required to go back to the first step and start with a new test. However, we should not write new tests until all the existing ones are passing.

In this phase, we are still in the *red* stage. While the code that was written would probably pass all the tests, that assumption is not yet confirmed.

Run all the tests

It is very important that all the tests are run and not only the last test that was written. The code that we just wrote might have made the last test pass while breaking something else. Running all the tests confirms not only that the implementation of the last test is correct, but also that it did not break the integrity of the application as a whole. This slow execution of the whole test suite is a sign of poorly written tests or having too much coupling in the code. Coupling prevents the easy isolation of external dependencies; thus, increasing the time required for the execution of tests.

In this phase, we are in the *green* state. All the tests are passing and the application behaves as we expect it to behave.

Refactor

While all the previous steps are mandatory, this one is optional. Even though refactoring is rarely done at the end of each cycle, sooner or later it will be desired, if not mandatory. Not every implementation of a test requires refactoring. There is no rule that tells you when to refactor and when not to. The best time is as soon as one gets a feeling that the code can be rewritten in a better or more optimum way.

What constitutes a candidate for refactoring? This is a hard question to answer since it can have many answers: it's hard to understand code, the illogical location of a piece of code, duplication, names that do not clearly state a purpose, long methods, classes that do too many things, and so on. The list can go on and on. No matter what the reasons are, the most important rule is that refactoring cannot change any existing functionality.

Repeat

Once all the steps (with *refactor* being optional) are finished, we repeat them. At first glance, the whole process might seem too long or too complicated, but it is not. Experienced TDD practitioners write one to ten lines of code before switching to the next step. The whole cycle should last anything between a couple of seconds and no more than a few minutes. If it takes more than that, the scope of a test is too big and should be split into smaller chunks. Be fast, fail fast, correct, and repeat.

With this knowledge in mind, let us go through the requirements of the application we're about to develop using the *red-green-refactor process*.

The Tic-Tac-Toe game requirements

Tic-Tac-Toe is most often played by young children. The rules of the game are fairly simple.

> Tic-tac-toe is a paper-and-pencil game for two players, X and O, who take turns marking the spaces in a 3×3 grid. The player who succeeds in placing three respective marks in a horizontal, vertical, or diagonal row, wins the game.
>
> For more information about the game, please visit Wikipedia (http://en.wikipedia.org/wiki/Tic-tac-toe).

More detailed requirements will be presented later on.

The exercise consists of a creation of a single test that corresponds to one of the requirements. The test is followed by the code that fulfills the expectations of that test. Finally, if needed, code is refactored. The same procedure should be repeated with more tests related to the same requirement. Once we're satisfied with tests and the implementation of that requirement, we'll move to the next one until they're all done.

In real-world situations, you wouldn't get such detailed requirements, but dive right into tests that would act as both requirements and validation. However, until you get comfortable with TDD, we'll have to define requirements in separation from tests.

Even though all the tests and the implementation are provided below, try to read only one requirement at a time and write test(s) and implementation code yourself. Once done, compare your solution with the one from this book and move to the next requirement. There is no one and only one solution—yours might be better than the ones presented here.

Developing Tic-Tac-Toe

Are you ready to code? Let's start with the first requirement.

Requirement 1

We should start by defining the boundaries and what constitutes an invalid placement of a piece.

 A piece can be placed on any empty space of a 3×3 board.

We can split this requirement into three tests:

- When a piece is placed anywhere outside the X axis, then RuntimeException is thrown.

- When a piece is placed anywhere outside the Y axis, then RuntimeException is thrown.

- When a piece is placed on an occupied space, then RuntimeException is thrown.

As you can see, the tests related to this first requirement are all about validations of the input argument. There is nothing in the requirements that says what should be done with those pieces.

Before we proceed with the first test, a brief explanation of how to test exceptions with JUnit is in order.

Starting from the release 4.7, JUnit introduced a feature called **Rule**. It can be used to do many different things (more information can be found at `https://github.com/junit-team/junit/wiki/Rules`), but in our case we're interested in the `ExpectedException` rule:

```
public class FooTest {
  @Rule
  public ExpectedException exception =
    ExpectedException.none();

  @Test
  public void whenDoFooThenThrowRuntimeException() {
    Foo foo = new Foo();
    exception.expect(RuntimeException.class);
    foo.doFoo();
  }
}
```

In this example, we defined that the `ExpectedException` is a rule. Later on, in the `doFooThrowsRuntimeException` test, we're specifying that we are expecting the `RuntimeException` to be thrown after the `Foo` class is instantiated. If it is thrown before, the test will fail. If the exception is thrown after, the test is successful.

`@Before` can be used to annotate a method that should be run before each test. It is a very useful feature with which we can, for example, instantiate a class used in tests or perform some other types of actions that should be run before each test:

```
private Foo foo;

@Before
public final void before() {
    foo = new Foo();
}
```

In this example, the `Foo` class will be instantiated before each test. This way, we can avoid having repetitive code that would instantiate `Foo` inside each `test` method.

Each test should be annotated with @Test. This tells JunitRunner which methods constitute tests. Each of them will be run in a random order so make sure that each test is self-sufficient and does not depend on the state that might be created by other tests:

```
@Test
public void whenSomethingThenResultIsSomethingElse() {
  // This is a test method
}
```

With this knowledge, you should be able to write your first test and follow it with the implementation. Once done, compare it with the solution provided below.

Use descriptive names for test methods

One of the benefits is that it helps to understand the objective of tests.

Using method names that describe tests is beneficial when trying to figure out why some tests failed or when the coverage should be increased with more tests. It should be clear what conditions are set before the test, what actions are performed, and what the expected outcome is.

There are many different ways to name test methods. My preferred method is to name them using the given/when/then syntax used in BDD scenarios. Given describes (pre)conditions, When describes actions, and Then describes the expected outcome. If a test does not have preconditions (usually set using the @Before and @BeforeClass annotations), Given can be skipped.

Do NOT rely only on comments to provide information about test objectives. Comments do not appear when tests are executed from your favorite IDE, nor do they appear in reports generated by the CI or build tools.

Besides writing tests, you'll need to run them as well. Since we are using Gradle, they can be run from the command prompt:

```
$ gradle test
```

IntelliJ IDEA provides a very good Gradle tasks model that can be reached by clicking on **View | Tool Windows | Gradle**. It lists all the tasks that can be run with Gradle (test being one of them).

The choice is yours—you can run tests in any way you see fit, as long as you run all of them.

Test

We should start by checking whether a piece is placed within the boundaries of the 3x3 board:

```
package com.packtpublishing.tddjava.ch03tictactoe;

import org.junit.Before;
import org.junit.Rule;
import org.junit.Test;
import org.junit.rules.ExpectedException;

public class TicTacToeSpec {

    @Rule
    public ExpectedException exception =
    ExpectedException.none();
    private TicTacToe ticTacToe;

    @Before
    public final void before() {
        ticTacToe = new TicTacToe();
    }

    @Test
    public void whenXOutsideBoardThenRuntimeException()
        {
      exception.expect(RuntimeException.class);
      ticTacToe.play(5, 2);

    }

}
```

 When a piece is placed anywhere outside the X axis, then `RuntimeException` is thrown.

In this test, we are defining that `RuntimeException` is expected when the `ticTacToe.play(5, 2)` method is invoked. It's a very short and easy test, and making it pass should be easy as well. All we have to do is create the `play` method and make sure that it throws `RuntimeException` when x argument is smaller than 1 or bigger than 3 (the board is 3x3). You should run this test three times. The first time, it should fail because the `play` method doesn't exist. Once it is added, it should fail because `RuntimeException` is not thrown. The third time, it should be successful because the code that corresponds with this test is fully implemented.

Implementation

Now that we have a clear definition of when an `Exception` should be thrown, the implementation should be straightforward:

```
package com.packtpublishing.tddjava.ch03tictactoe;

public class TicTacToe {

    public void play(int x, int y) {
        if (x < 1 || x > 3) {
            throw
            new RuntimeException("X is outside board");
        }
    }

}
```

As you can see, this code does not contain anything else, but the bare minimum required for the test to pass.

 Some TDD practitioners tend to take *minimum* as a literal meaning. They would have the `play` method with only the `throw new RuntimeException();` line. I tend to translate *minimum* to *as little as possible within reason*.

We're not adding numbers, nor are we returning anything. It's all about doing small changes very fast (remember the game of ping pong?). For now, we're doing red-green steps. There's not much we can do to improve this code so we're skipping the refactoring.

Let's move onto the next test.

Test

This test is almost the same as the previous one. This time we should validate the Y axis:

```
@Test
public void whenYOutsideBoardThenRuntimeException() {
    exception.expect(RuntimeException.class);
    ticTacToe.play(2, 5);
}
```

When a piece is placed anywhere outside the Y axis, then
RuntimeException is thrown.

Implementation

The implementation of this specification is almost the same as the previous one.
All we have to do is throw an Exception if Y does not fall within the defined range:

```
public void play(int x, int y) {
if (x < 1 || x > 3) {
    throw
    new RuntimeException("X is outside board");
} else if (y < 1 || y > 3) {
    throw
    new RuntimeException("X is outside board");
}
}
```

In order for the last test to pass, we had to add the *else* clause that checks
whether Y is inside the board.

Let's do the last test for this requirement.

Test

Now that we know that pieces are placed within the board's boundaries, we should
make sure that they can be placed only on unoccupied spaces:

```
@Test
public void whenOccupiedThenRuntimeException() {
    ticTacToe.play(2, 1);
    exception.expect(RuntimeException.class);
    ticTacToe.play(2, 1);
}
```

When a piece is placed on an occupied space, then
RuntimeException is thrown.

That's it; this was our last test. Once the implementation is finished, we can consider
the first requirement as done.

Implementation

To implement the last test, we should store the location of the placed pieces in an array. Every time a new piece is placed, we should verify that the place is not occupied, or else throw an exception:

```
private Character[][] board = {{'\0', '\0', '\0'},
{'\0', '\0', \0'}, {'\0', '\0', '\0'}};

public void play(int x, int y) {
    if (x < 1 || x > 3) {
        throw
        new RuntimeException("X is outside board");
    } else if (y < 1 || y > 3) {
        throw
        new RuntimeException("Y is outside board");
    }
    if (board[x - 1][y - 1] != '\0') {
        throw
        new RuntimeException("Box is occupied");
    } else {
        board[x - 1][y - 1] = 'X';
    }
}
```

We're checking whether a place that was played is occupied and, if it is not, we're changing the array entry value from empty (\0) to occupied (X). Keep in mind that we're still not storing who played (X or O).

Refactoring

While the code that we did by now fulfills the requirements set by the tests, it looks a bit confusing. If someone read it, it would not be clear as to what the play method does. We should refactor it by moving the code into separate methods. The refactored code will look like the following:

```
public void play(int x, int y) {
    checkAxis(x);
    checkAxis(y);
    setBox(x, y);
}

private void checkAxis(int axis) {
    if (axis < 1 || axis > 3) {
        throw
        new RuntimeException("X is outside board");
    }
}
```

```
    private void setBox(int x, int y) {
        if (board[x - 1][y - 1] != '\0') {
            throw
            new RuntimeException("Box is occupied");
        } else {
            board[x - 1][y - 1] = 'X';
        }
    }
}
```

With this refactoring, we did not change the functionality of the `play` method. It behaves exactly the same as it behaved before, but the new code is a bit more readable. Since we had tests that covered all the existing functionality, there was no fear that we might do something wrong. As long as all tests are passing all the time and refactoring did not introduce any new behavior, it is safe to do changes to the code.

The source code can be found in the `01-exceptions` branch of the `tdd-java-ch03-tic-tac-toe` Git repository at https://bitbucket.org/vfarcic/tdd-java-ch03-tic-tac-toe/branch/01-exceptions.

Requirement 2

Now it's time to work on the specification of which player is about to play his turn.

 [There should be a way to find out which player should play next.]

We can split this requirement into three tests:

- The first turn should be played by played x
- If the last turn was played by x, then the next turn should be played by o
- If the last turn was played by o, then the next turn should be played by x

Until this moment, we haven't used any of the JUnit's asserts. To use them, we need to import the `static` methods from the `org.junit.Assert` class:

```
import static org.junit.Assert.*;
```

In their essence, methods inside the `Assert` class are very simple. Most of them start with `assert`. For example, `assertEquals` compares two objects: `assertNotEquals` verifies that two objects are not the same and `assertArrayEquals` verifies that two arrays are the same. Each of those asserts has many overloaded variations so that almost any type of Java objects can be used.

In our case, we'll need to compare two characters. The first is the one we're expecting and the second one is the actual character retrieved from the `nextPlayer` method.

Now it's time to write those tests and the implementation.

Write the test before writing the implementation code

The benefits of doing this are as follows: it ensures that testable code is written and ensures that every line of code gets tests written for it.

By writing or modifying the test first, the developer is focused on requirements before starting to work on a code. This is the main difference when compared to writing tests after the implementation is done. An additional benefit is that with tests first, we are avoiding the danger that the tests work as quality checking instead of quality assurance.

Test

The player X has the first turn:

```
@Test
public void givenFirstTurnWhenNextPlayerThenX() {
    assertEquals('X', ticTacToe.nextPlayer());
}
```

 The first turn should be played by player X.

This test should be self-explanatory. We are expecting the `nextPlayer` method to return X. If you try to run this, you'll see that the code does not even compile. That's because the `nextPlayer` method does not even exist. Our job is to write the `nextPlayer` method and make sure that it returns the correct value.

Implementation

There's no real need to check whether it really is the player's first turn or not. As it stands, this test can be fulfilled by always returning X. Later tests will force us to refine this code:

```
public char nextPlayer() {
    return 'X';
}
```

Test

Now, we should make sure that players are changing. After x is finished, it should be O's turn, then again x, and so on:

```
@Test
public void givenLastTurnWasXWhenNextPlayerThenO()
{
    ticTacToe.play(1, 1);
    assertEquals('O', ticTacToe.nextPlayer());
}
```

 If the last turn was played by X, then the next turn should be played by O.

Implementation

In order to track who should play next, we need to store who played last:

```
private char lastPlayer = '\0';

public void play(int x, int y) {
    checkAxis(x);
    checkAxis(y);
    setBox(x, y);
    lastPlayer = nextPlayer();
}

public char nextPlayer() {
    if (lastPlayer == 'X') {
        return 'O';
    }
    return 'X';
}
```

You are probably starting to get the hang of it. Tests are small and easy to write. With enough experience, it should take a minute, if not seconds, to write a test and as much time or less to write the implementation.

Test

Finally, we can check whether x's turn comes after O played.

 If the last turn was played by O, then the next turn should be played by X.

There's nothing to do to fulfill this test and, therefore, the test is useless and should be discarded. If you write this test, you'll discover that it is a false positive; it would pass without changing the implementation—try it out. Write this test and if it is successful without writing any implementation code, discard it.

The source code can be found in the `02-next-player` branch of the `tdd-java-ch03-tic-tac-toe` Git repository at `https://bitbucket.org/vfarcic/tdd-java-ch03-tic-tac-toe/branch/02-next-player`.

Requirement 3

It's time to work on winning the rules of the game. This is the part where, when compared with the previous code, work becomes a bit more tedious. We should check all the possible winning combinations and, if one of them is fulfilled, declare a winner.

 A player wins by being the first to connect a line of friendly pieces from one side or corner of the board to the other.

To check whether a line of friendly pieces is connected, we should verify horizontal, vertical, and diagonal lines.

Test

Let's start by defining the default response of the `play` method:

```
@Test
public void whenPlayThenNoWinner()
{
    String actual = ticTacToe.play(1,1);
    assertEquals("No winner", actual);
}
```

 If no winning condition is fulfilled, then there is no winner.

Implementation

The default return values are always easiest to implement and this one is
no exception:

```
public String play(int x, int y) {
    checkAxis(x);
    checkAxis(y);
    setBox(x, y);
    lastPlayer = nextPlayer();
    return "No winner";
}
```

Test

Now that we have declared what the default response is (no winner), it's time to start
working on different winning conditions:

```
@Test
public void whenPlayAndWholeHorizontalLineThenWinner() {
    ticTacToe.play(1, 1); // X
    ticTacToe.play(1, 2); // O
    ticTacToe.play(2, 1); // X
    ticTacToe.play(2, 2); // O
    String actual = ticTacToe.play(3, 1); // X
    assertEquals("X is the winner", actual);
}
```

 The player wins when the whole horizontal line is occupied by
his pieces.

Implementation

To fulfill this test, we need to check whether any horizontal line is filled by the same
mark as the current player. Until this moment, we didn't care what was put to the
board array. Now, we need to introduce not only which board boxes are empty,
but also which player played them:

```
public String play(int x, int y) {
    checkAxis(x);
    checkAxis(y);
    lastPlayer = nextPlayer();
```

```
        setBox(x, y, lastPlayer);
        for (int index = 0; index < 3; index++) {
            if (board[0][index] == lastPlayer &&
                    board[1][index] == lastPlayer &&
                    board[2][index] == lastPlayer) {
                return lastPlayer + " is the winner";
            }
        }
        return "No winner";
    }
    private void setBox(int x, int y, char lastPlayer)
{
    if (board[x - 1][y - 1] != '\0') {
        throw
        new RuntimeException("Box is occupied");
    } else {
        board[x - 1][y - 1] = lastPlayer;
    }
}
}
```

Refactoring

The preceding code satisfies the tests, but is not necessarily the final version. It served its purpose of getting code coverage as fast as possible. Now, since we have tests that guarantee the integrity of the expected behavior, we can refactor the code:

```
    private static final int SIZE = 3;
    public String play(int x, int y) {
        checkAxis(x);
        checkAxis(y);
        lastPlayer = nextPlayer();
        setBox(x, y, lastPlayer);
        if (isWin()) {
            return lastPlayer + " is the winner";
        }
        return "No winner";
    }

    private boolean isWin() {
    for (int i = 0; i < SIZE; i++) {
        if (board[0][i] + board[1][i] + board[2][i]
          == (lastPlayer * SIZE)) {
           return true;
          }
        }
        return false;
    }
```

This refactored solution looks better. The `play` method keeps being short and easy to understand. Winning logic is moved to a separate method. Not only have we kept the `play` method's purpose clear, but this separation also allows us to grow the winning condition's code in separation from the rest.

Test

We should also check whether there is a win by filling the vertical line:

```
@Test
public void whenPlayAndWholeVerticalLineThenWinner() {
    ticTacToe.play(2, 1); // X
    ticTacToe.play(1, 1); // O
    ticTacToe.play(3, 1); // X
    ticTacToe.play(1, 2); // O
    ticTacToe.play(2, 2); // X
    String actual = ticTacToe.play(1, 3); // O
    assertEquals("O is the winner", actual);
}
```

 The player wins when the whole vertical line is occupied by his pieces.

Implementation

This implementation should be similar to the previous one. We already have horizontal verification and now we need to do the same vertically:

```
private boolean isWin() {
 int playerTotal = lastPlayer * 3;
 for (int i = 0; i < SIZE; i++) {
     if (board[0][i] + board[1][i] + board[2][i]
     == playerTotal) {
         return true;
     } else if (playerTotal == )
  {
         return true;
     }
 }
 return false;
}
```

Test

Now that horizontal and vertical lines are covered, we should move our attention to diagonal combinations:

```
@Test
public void whenPlayAndTopBottomDiagonalLineThenWinner() {
    ticTacToe.play(1, 1); // X
    ticTacToe.play(1, 2); // O
    ticTacToe.play(2, 2); // X
    ticTacToe.play(1, 3); // O
    String actual = ticTacToe.play(3, 3); // O
    assertEquals("X is the winner", actual);
}
```

 The player wins when the whole diagonal line from the top-left to bottom-right is occupied by his pieces.

Implementation

Since there is only one line that can constitute with a requirement, we can check it directly without any loops:

```
private boolean isWin() {
  int playerTotal = lastPlayer * 3;
  for (int i = 0; i < SIZE; i++) {
      if (board[0][i] + board[1][i] + board[2][i]
      playerTotal) {
          return true;
      } else if (playerTotal == )
{
          return true;
      }
  }
  if ((board[0][0] + board[1][1] + board[2][2])
  == playerTotal) {
      return true;
  }
  return false;
}
```

Test

Finally, there is the last possible winning condition to tackle:

```
@Test
public void whenPlayAndBottomTopDiagonalLineThenWinner() {
    ticTacToe.play(1, 3); // X
    ticTacToe.play(1, 1); // O
    ticTacToe.play(2, 2); // X
    ticTacToe.play(1, 2); // O
    String actual = ticTacToe.play(3, 1); // O
    assertEquals("X is the winner", actual);
}
```

 The player wins when the whole diagonal line from the bottom-left to top-right is occupied by his pieces

Implementation

The implementation of this test should be almost the same as the previous one:

```
private boolean isWin() {
  int playerTotal = lastPlayer * 3;
  for (int i = 0; i < SIZE; i++) {
      if (board[0][i] + board[1][i] + board[2][i]
      playerTotal) {
          return true;
      } else if (playerTotal == )
{
          return true;
      }
  }
  if ((board[0][0] + board[1][1] + board[2][2])
  == playerTotal) {
      return true;
  } else if (playerTotal == (board[0][2] + board[1][1] +
    board[2][0])) {
      return true;
  }
  return false;
}
```

Refactoring

The way we're handling possible diagonal wins, the calculation doesn't look right. Maybe the reutilization of the existing loop would make more sense:

```
private boolean isWin() {
    int playerTotal = lastPlayer * 3;
    char diagonal1 = '\0';
    char diagonal2 = '\0';
    for (int i = 0; i < SIZE; i++) {
        diagonal1 += board[i][i];
        diagonal2 += board[i][SIZE - i - 1];
        if (board[0][i] + board[1][i] + board[2][i]) ==
          playerTotal) {
            return true;
        } else if (playerTotal == ) {
            return true;
        }
    }
    if (diagonal1 == playerTotal || diagonal2 == playerTotal) {
        return true;
    }
    return false;
}
```

The source code can be found in the `03-wins` branch of the `tdd-java-ch03-tic-tac-toe` Git repository at `https://bitbucket.org/vfarcic/tdd-java-ch03-tic-tac-toe/branch/03-wins`.

Now, let's go through the last requirement.

Requirement 4

The only thing missing is how to tackle the draw result.

 The result is a draw when all the boxes are filled.

Test

We can test the draw result by filling all the board's boxes:

```
@Test
public void whenAllBoxesAreFilledThenDraw() {
    ticTacToe.play(1, 1);
    ticTacToe.play(1, 2);
    ticTacToe.play(1, 3);
    ticTacToe.play(2, 1);
    ticTacToe.play(2, 3);
    ticTacToe.play(2, 2);
    ticTacToe.play(3, 1);
    ticTacToe.play(3, 3);
    String actual = ticTacToe.play(3, 2);
    assertEquals("The result is draw", actual);
}
```

Implementation

Checking whether it's a draw is fairly straightforward. All we have to do is check whether all the board's boxes are filled. We can do that by iterating through the board array:

```
public String play(int x, int y) {
    checkAxis(x);
    checkAxis(y);
    lastPlayer = nextPlayer();
    setBox(x, y, lastPlayer);
    if (isWin()) {
        return lastPlayer + " is the winner";
    } else if (isDraw()) {
        return "The result is draw";
    } else {
        return "No winner";
    }
}

private boolean isDraw() {
    for (int x = 0; x < SIZE; x++) {
        for (int y = 0; y < SIZE; y++) {
            if (board[x][y] == '\0') {
                return false;
            }
        }
    }
    return true;
}
```

Refactoring

Even though the isWin method is not the scope of the last test, it can still be refactored even more. For one, we don't need to check all the combinations, but only those related to the position of the last piece played. The final version could look like the following:

```java
private boolean isWin(int x, int y) {
    int playerTotal = lastPlayer * 3;
    char horizontal, vertical, diagonal1, diagonal2;
    horizontal = vertical = diagonal1 = diagonal2 = '\0';
    for (int i = 0; i < SIZE; i++) {
        horizontal += board[i][y - 1];
        vertical += board[x - 1][i];
        diagonal1 += board[i][i];
        diagonal2 += board[i][SIZE - i - 1];
    }
    if (horizontal == playerTotal
            || vertical == playerTotal
            || diagonal1 == playerTotal
            || diagonal2 == playerTotal) {
        return true;
    }
    return false;
}
```

Refactoring can be done on any part of the code at any time, as long as all the tests are successful. While it's often easiest and fastest to refactor the code that was just written, going back to something that was written the other day, previous month, or even years ago, is more than welcome. The best moment to refactor something is when someone sees an opportunity to make it better. It doesn't matter who wrote it or when; making the code better is always a good thing to do.

The source code can be found in the 04-draw branch of the tdd-java-ch03-tic-tac-toe Git repository at https://bitbucket.org/vfarcic/tdd-java-ch03-tic-tac-toe/branch/04-draw.

Code coverage

We did not use code coverage tools throughout this exercise. The reason is that we wanted you to be focused on the red-green-refactor model. You wrote a test, saw it fail, wrote the implementation code, saw that all the tests were executed successfully, refactored the code whenever you saw an opportunity to make it better, and then you repeated the process. Did our tests cover all cases? That's something that **code coverage** tools such as JaCoCo can answer. Should you use those tools? Probably, only in the beginning. Let me clarify that. When you are starting with TDD, you will probably miss some tests or implement more than what the tests defined. In those cases, using code coverage is a good way to learn from your own mistakes. Later on, the more experienced you become with TDD, the less of a need you'll have for such tools. You'll write tests and just enough of the code to make them pass. Your coverage will be high with or without tools such as JaCoCo. There will be a small amount of code not covered by tests because you'll make a conscious decision about what is not worth testing.

Tools such as JaCoCo were designed mostly as a way to verify that the tests written after the implementation code are providing enough coverage. With TDD, we are taking a different approach with the inverted order (tests before the implementation).

Still, we suggest you use JaCoCo as a learning tool and decide for yourself whether to use it in the future.

To enable JaCoCo within Gradle, add the following to the `build.gradle`:

```
apply plugin: 'jacoco'
```

From now on, Gradle will collect JaCoCo metrics every time we run tests. Those metrics can be transformed into a nice report using the `jacocoTestReport` Gradle target. Let's run our tests again and see what the code coverage is:

```
$ gradle clean test jacocoTestReport
```

The end result is the report located in the `build/reports/jacoco/test/html` directory. Results will vary depending on the solution you made for this exercise. My results say that there is a 100 percent of instructions coverage and 96 percent of branches coverage; 4 percent is missing because there was no test case where the player played on a box 0 or negative. The implementation of that case is there, but there is no specific test that covers it. Overall, this is a pretty good coverage.

JaCoCo will be added in the source code. This is found in the `05-jacoco` branch of the `tdd-java-ch03-tic-tac-toe` Git repository at `https://bitbucket.org/vfarcic/tdd-java-ch03-tic-tac-toe/branch/05-jacoco`.

More exercises

We just developed one (most commonly used) variation of the Tic-Tac-Toe game. As an additional exercise, pick one or more variations from Wikipedia (`http://en.wikipedia.org/wiki/Tic-tac-toe`) and implement it using the red-green-refactor procedure. When finished, implement a kind of AI that would play O's turns. Since Tic-Tac-Toe usually leads to a draw, AI can be considered finished when it successfully reaches a draw for any combination of X's moves.

While working on those exercises, remember to be fast and play ping pong. Also, most of all, remember to use the red-green-refactor procedure.

Summary

We managed to finish the Tic-Tac-Toe game using the red-green-refactor process. The examples themselves were simple and you probably didn't have a problem following them.

The objective of this chapter was not to dive into something complicated (that comes later), but to get into the habit of using short a and repetitive cycle called red-green-refactor.

We learned that the easiest way to develop something is by splitting it into very small chunks. Design was emerging from tests instead of using a big up-front approach. No line of the implementation code was written without writing a test first and seeing it fail. By confirming that the last test fails, we are confirming that it is valid (it's easy to make a mistake and write a test that is always successful) and the feature we are about to implement does not exist. After the test failed, we wrote the implementation of that test. While writing the implementation, we tried to make it a minimal one with the objective to make the test pass, not to make the solution final. We were repeating this process until we felt that there was a need to refactor the code. Refactoring did not introduce any new functionality (we did not change what the application does), but made the code more optimum and easier to read and maintain.

In the next chapter, we'll elaborate in more detail about what constitutes a unit within the context of TDD and how to approach the creation of tests based on those units.

Unit Testing – Focusing on What You Do and Not on What Has Been Done

"To create something exceptional, your mindset must be relentlessly focused on the smallest detail."

- Giorgio Armani

As promised, each chapter will explore a different Java testing framework and this one is no exception. We'll use TestNG to build our specifications.

In the previous chapter, we practiced the red-green-refactor procedure. We used unit tests without going deeper into how unit testing works in the context of TDD. We'll build on the knowledge from the last chapter and go into more detail by trying to explain what unit tests really are and how they fit in to the TDD approach to build software.

The goal of this chapter is to learn how to focus on the unit we're currently working on and how to ignore or isolate those that were done before.

Once we're comfortable with TestNG and unit testing, we'll dive right into the requirements of our next application and start coding.

The following topics will be covered in this chapter:

- Unit testing
- Unit testing with TDD
- TestNG
- Remote-controlled ship requirements
- Developing the remote-controlled ship
- Summary

Unit testing

Frequent manual testing is too impractical to any but the smallest systems. The only way around this is the usage of automated tests. They are the only effective method to reduce the time and cost of building, deploying, and maintaining applications. In order to effectively manage applications, it is of the utmost importance that both the implementation and test code are as simple as possible. Simplicity is one of the core Extreme Programming (XP) values (`http://www.extremeprogramming.org/rules/simple.html`) and the key to TDD and programming in general. It is most often accomplished through division into small units. In Java, units are methods. Being the smallest, feedback loop they provide is the fastest so we spend most of our time thinking and working on them. As a counterpart to implementation methods, unit tests should constitute by far the biggest percentage of all tests.

What is unit testing?

Unit testing (UT) is a practice that forces us to test small, individual and isolated units of code. They are usually methods even though in some cases classes or even whole applications can be considered units, as well. In order to write UT, code under tests needs to be isolated from the rest of the application. Preferably, that isolation is already ingrained in the code or it can be accomplished with the usage of mocks (more on mocks will be covered in *Chapter 6, Mocking - Removing External Dependencies*). If unit tests of a particular method cross the boundaries of that unit, then they become integration tests. As such, it becomes less clear what is under tests. In case of a failure, the scope of a problem suddenly increases and finding the cause becomes more tedious.

Why unit testing?

A common question, especially within organizations that rely heavily on manual testing, is *why should we use unit instead of functional and integration testing?* This question in itself is flawed. Unit testing does not replace other types of testing. Instead, unit testing reduces the scope of other types of tests. By its nature, unit tests are easier and faster to write than any other type of tests, thus, reducing the cost and time-to-market. Due to the reduced time to write and run them, they tend to detect problems much sooner. The faster we detect problems, the cheaper it is to fix them. A bug that was detected minutes after it was created is much easier to fix than if that same bug was found days, weeks, or even months after it was made.

Code refactoring

Code refactoring is the process of changing the structure of an existing code without changing its external behavior. The purpose of refactoring is to improve an existing code. This improvement can be for many different reasons. We might want to make the code more readable, less complex, easier to maintain, cheaper to extend, and so on. No matter what the reason for refactoring is, the ultimate goal is always to make it better in one way or another. The effect of this goal is a reduction in technical debt; a reduction in pending work that needs to be done due to suboptimal design, architecture, or coding.

Typically, we approach refactoring by applying a set of small changes without modifying intended behavior. Reducing the scope of refactoring changes, allows us to continuously confirm that those changes did not break any existing functionality. The only way to effectively obtain this confirmation is through the usage of automated tests.

One of the great benefits of unit tests is that they are the best refactoring enablers. Refactoring is too risky when there are no automated tests to confirm that the application still behaves as expected. While any type of tests can be used to provide code coverage required for refactoring, in most cases only unit tests can provide the required level of details.

Why not use unit tests exclusively?

At this moment, you might be wondering whether unit testing could provide a solution for all your testing needs. Unfortunately, that is not the case. While unit tests usually cover the biggest percentage of your testing needs, functional and integration tests should be an integral part of your testing toolbox.

We'll cover other types of tests in more detail in later chapters. For now, a few important distinctions between them are as follows:

- **Unit tests** try to verify small units of functionality. In the Java world, those units are methods. All external dependencies such as invocations of other classes and methods or database calls should be done in memory with the usage of mocks, stubs, spies, fakes, and dummies. *Gerard Meszaros* coined a more general term "test doubles" that envelops all those (`http://en.wikipedia.org/wiki/Test_double`).

  Unit tests are simple, easy to write, and fast to run. They are usually the biggest percentage of a testing suite.

- **Functional and acceptance** tests have a job to verify that the application we're building works as expected, as a whole. While those two differ in their purpose, both share a similar goal. Unlike unit tests that are verifying the internal quality of the code, functional and acceptance tests are trying to ensure that the system is working correctly from the customer's or user's point of view. Those tests are usually smaller in number when compared with unit tests due to the cost and effort needed to both write and run them.

- **Integration** tests intend to verify that separate units, modules, applications, or even whole systems are properly integrated with each other. You might have a frontend application that uses backend APIs that, in turn, communicate with a database. The job of integration tests would be to verify that all three of those separate components of the system are indeed integrated and can communicate with each other. Since we already know that all the units are working and all functional and acceptance tests are passed, integration tests are usually the smallest of all three as their job is only to confirm that all the pieces are working well together.

The testing pyramid states that you should have many more unit tests than higher level tests (UI tests, integration tests, and so on). Why is that? Unit tests are much cheaper to write, faster to run, and, at the same time, provide much bigger coverage. Take, for example, registration functionality. We should test what happens when a username is empty, when a password is empty, when a username or password is not in the correct format, when the user already exists, and so on. Only for this single functionality there can be tens, if not hundreds of tests. Writing and running all those tests from the UI can be very expensive (time-consuming to write and slow to run). On the other hand, unit testing a method that does this validation is easy, fast to write, and fast to run. If all those cases are covered with unit tests, we could be satisfied with a single integration test that checks whether our UI is calling the correct method on the backend. If it is, details are irrelevant from an integration point of view since we know that all cases are already covered on the unit level.

Unit testing with TDD

What is the difference in the way we write unit tests in the context of TDD? The major differentiator is in *when*. While traditionally unit tests are written after the implementation code is done, in TDD we write tests before—the order of things is inverted. Without TDD, the purpose of unit tests is to validate an existing code. TDD teaches us that unit tests should drive our development and design. They should define the behavior of the smallest possible unit. They are micro requirements pending to be developed. A test tells you what to do next and when you're done doing it. Depending on the type of tests (unit, functional, integration, and so on), the scope of what should be done next differs. In the case of TDD with unit tests, this scope is the smallest possible, meaning a method or, more often, a part of it. Moreover, with TDD driven with unit tests, we are forced to comply to some design principles such as **KISS** (**keep it simple stupid**). By writing simple tests with a very small scope, the implementation of those tests tends to be simple as well. By forcing tests not to use external dependencies, we are forcing the implementation code to have separation of concerns well designed. There are many other examples of how TDD helps us to write better code. Those same benefits cannot be accomplished with unit testing alone. Without TDD, unit tests are forced to work with an existing code and have no influence on the design.

To summarize, the main goal of unit testing without TDD is the validation of the existing code. Unit testing written in advance using test-driven development procedure has the main objective specification and design with validation being a side product. This side product is often of a higher quality than when tests are written after the implementation.

TDD forces us to think through our requirements and design, write clean code that works, create executable requirements, and refactor safely and often. On top of all that, we end up with high test code coverage that is used to regression test all our code whenever some change is introduced. Unit testing without TDD gives us only tests and, often, with doubtful quality.

TestNG

JUnit and TestNG are two major Java testing frameworks. You already wrote tests with JUnit in the previous chapter and, hopefully, got a good understanding of how it works. How about TestNG? It was born out of a desire to make JUnit better. Indeed, it contains some functionalities that JUnit doesn't have.

The following subchapters summarize some of the differences between the two of them. We'll try not only to provide an explanation of differences, but also their evaluation in the context of unit testing with TDD.

The @Test annotation

Both JUnit and TestNG use the @Test annotation to specify which method is considered to be a test. Unlike JUnit, which requires every method to be annotated with @Test, TestNG allows us to use this annotation on a class level, as well. When used in this way, all public methods are considered tests unless specified otherwise:

```
@Test
public class DirectionSpec {

    public void whenGetFromShortNameNThenReturnDirectionN() {
        Direction direction = Direction.getFromShortName('N');
        assertEquals(direction, Direction.NORTH);
    }

    public void whenGetFromShortNameWThenReturnDirectionW() {
        Direction direction = Direction.getFromShortName('W');
        assertEquals(direction, Direction.WEST);
    }

}
```

In this example, we put the `@Test` annotation above the `DirectionSpec` class. As a result, both the `whenGetFromShortNameNThenReturnDirectionN` and `whenGetFromShortNameWThenReturnDirectionW` methods are considered tests. If that code was written using JUnit, both the methods would need to have the `@Test` annotation.

The @BeforeSuite, @BeforeTest, @BeforeGroups, @AfterGroups, @AfterTest, and @AfterSuite annotations

Those four annotations do not have their equivalents in JUnit. TestNG can group tests into suites, using XML configuration. Methods annotated with `@BeforeSuite` and `@AfterSuite` are run before and after all the tests in the specified suite have run. Similarly, the `@BeforeTest` and `@AfterTest` annotated methods are run before any test method belonging to the test classes has run. Finally, TestNG tests can be organized into groups. The `@BeforeGroups` and `@AfterGroups` annotations allows us to run methods before the first test and after the last test, in specified groups, is run.

While those annotations can be very useful when tests are written after the implementation code, they do not provide much usage in the context of TDD. Unlike traditional testing, which is often planned and written as a separate project, TDD teaches us to write one test at a time and keep everything simple. Most importantly, unit tests are supposed to run fast so there is no need to group them into suites or groups. When tests are fast, running anything less than everything is a waste. If, for example, all tests are run in less than 15 seconds, there is no need to run only a part of them. On the other hand, when tests are slow, it is often a sign that external dependencies are not isolated. No matter what the reason is behind slow tests, the solution is not to run only a part of them, but to fix the problem.

Moreover, functional and integration tests do tend to be slower and require us to have some kind of separation. However, it is better to separate them in, for example, `build.gradle` so that each type of test is run as a separate task.

The @BeforeClass and @AfterClass annotations

These annotations have the same function in both JUnit and TestNG. Annotated methods will be run before the first test and after the last test, in a current class, are run. The only difference is that TestNG does not require those methods to be static. The reason behind this can be found in the different approaches those two frameworks take when running test methods. JUnit isolates each test into its own instance of the test class, forcing us to have those methods defined as static and, therefore, reusable across all test runs. TestNG, on the other hand, executes all test methods in the context of a single test class instance eliminating the need for those methods to be static.

The @BeforeMethod and @AfterMethod annotations

The `@Before` and `@After` annotations are equivalent to JUnit. Annotated methods are run before and after each test method.

The @Test(enable = false) annotation argument

Both JUnit and TestNG can disable tests. While JUnit uses a separate `@Ignore` annotation, TestNG uses the `@Test` annotation Boolean argument `enable`. Functionally, both work in the same way and the difference is only in the way we write them.

The @Test(expectedExceptions = SomeClass.class) annotation argument

This is the case where JUnit has the advantage. While both provide the same way to specify the expected exception (in the case of JUnit, argument is called simply expected), JUnit introduces rules that are a more elegant way to test exceptions (we already worked with them in *Chapter 2, Tools, Frameworks, and Environment*).

TestNG vs JUnit summary

There are many other differences between those two frameworks. For brevity, we did not cover all of them in this book. Consult their documentation for further information.

 More information about JUnit and TestNG can be found at `http://junit.org/` and `http://testng.org/`.

TestNG provides more features and is more advanced than JUnit. We'll work with TestNG throughout this chapter, and you'll get to know it better. One thing that you'll notice is that we won't use any of those advanced features. The reason is that, with TDD, we rarely need them when working with unit tests. Functional and Integration tests are of a different kind and would serve as a better demonstration of TestNG's superiority. However, there are tools that are more suited for those types of tests, as you'll see in the following chapters.

Which one should you use? I'll leave that choice up to you. By the time you finish this chapter, you'll have hands-on knowledge of both JUnit and TestNG.

Remote controlled ship requirements

We'll work on a variation of a well-known kata called *Mars Rover*, originally published in *Dallas Hack Club* (`http://dallashackclub.com/rover`).

Imagine that a naval ship is placed somewhere on Earth's seas. Since this is the 21st century, we can control that ship remotely.

 Our job will be to create a program that can move the ship around the seas.

Since this is a TDD book and the subject of this chapter is unit tests, we'll develop an application using a test-driven development approach with focus on unit tests. In the previous chapter, you learned the theory and had practical experience with the red-green-refactor procedure. We'll build on top of that and try to learn how to effectively employ unit testing. Specifically, we'll try to concentrate on a unit we're developing and learn how to isolate and ignore dependencies that a unit might use. Not only that, but we'll try to concentrate on one requirement at a time. For this reason, you were presented only with high-level requirements; we should be able to move the remote-controlled ship, located somewhere on the planet, around.

To make things easier, all the supporting classes are already made and tested. This will allow us to concentrate on the main task at hand and, at the same time, keep this exercise concise.

Developing the remote-controlled ship

Let's start by importing the existing Git repository.

Project setup

Let's start setting up the project:

1. Open IntelliJ IDEA. If an existing project is already opened, select **File | Close Project**.

    You will be presented with a screen similar to the following:

    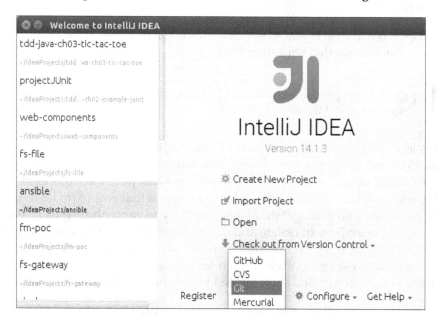

2. To import the project from the Git repository, click on **Check out from Version Control** and select **Git**. Type `https://bitbucket.org/vfarcic/tdd-java-ch04-ship.git` in to the **Git Repository URL** field and click on **Clone**:

    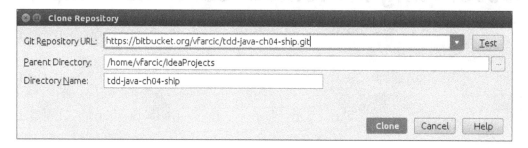

3. Answer **Yes** when asked whether you would like to open the project. Next you will be presented with the **Import Project from Gradle** dialog. Click on **OK**:

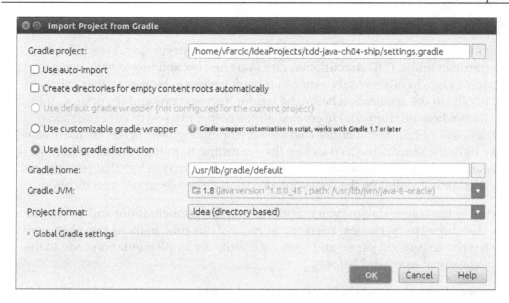

4. IDEA will need to spend some time downloading the dependencies specified in the buld.gradle file. Once that is done, you'll see that some classes and corresponding tests are already created:

Helper classes

Imagine that a colleague of yours started working on this project. He's a good programmer and a TDD practitioner, and you trust his abilities to have a good test code coverage. In other words, you can rely on his work. However, that colleague did not finish the application before he left for his vacations and it's up to you to continue where he stopped. He created all the helper classes: `Direction`, `Location`, `Planet`, and `Point`. You'll notice that the corresponding test classes are there as well. They have the same name as the class they're testing with the *Spec* suffix (that is, `DirectionSpec`). The reason for using this suffix is to make clear that tests are not intended only to validate the code, but also to serve as executable specification.

On top of the helper classes, you'll find the `Ship` (implementation) and `ShipSpec` (specifications/tests) classes. We'll spend most of our time in those two classes. We'll write tests in `ShipSpec` and then we'll write the implementation code in the `Ship` class (just as we did before).

Since we already learned that tests are not only used as a way to validate the code, but also as executable documentation, from this moment on, we'll use the phrase *specification* or *spec* instead of *test*.

Every time we finish writing a specification or the code that implements it, we'll run `gradle test` either from the command prompt or by using the Gradle projects IDEA Tool Window:

With project setup, we're ready to dive into the first requirement.

Requirement 1

We need to know what the current location of the ship is in order to be able to move it. Moreover, we should also know which direction it is facing: north, south, east, or west. Therefore, the first requirement is the following:

 You are given the initial starting point (**x**, **y**) of a ship and the direction (**N**, **S**, **E**, or **W**) it is facing.

Before we start working on this requirement, let's go through helper classes that can be used. The `Point` class holds the `x` and `y` coordinates. It has the following constructor:

```
public Point(int x, int y) {
    this.x = x;
    this.y = y;
}
```

Similarly, we have the `Direction` enum class with the following values:

```
public enum Direction {
    NORTH(0, 'N'),
    EAST(1, 'E'),
    SOUTH(2, 'S'),
    WEST(3, 'W'),
    NONE(4, 'X');
}
```

Finally, there is the `Location` class that requires both of those classes to be passed as constructor arguments:

```
public Location(Point point, Direction direction) {
    this.point = point;
    this.direction = direction;
}
```

Knowing this, it should be fairly easy to write a test for this first requirement. We should work in the same way as we did in the previous chapter.

Try to write specs by yourself. When done, compare it with the solution in this book. Repeat the same process with the code that implements specs. Try to write it by yourself and, once done, compare it with the solution we're proposing.

Specification

The specification for this requirement can be the following;

```
@Test
public class ShipSpec {

    public void whenInstantiatedThenLocationIsSet() {
        Location location = new Location(
        new Point(21, 13), Direction.NORTH);
        Ship ship = new Ship(location);
        assertEquals(ship.getLocation(), location);
    }
}
```

This was an easy one. We're just checking whether the Location object we're passing as the Ship constructor is stored and can be accessed through the location getter.

> **The @Test annotation**
> When TestNG has the @Test annotation set on the class level, there is no need to specify which methods should be used as tests. In this case, all public methods are considered to be TestNG tests.

Specification implementation

The implementation of this specification should be fairly easy. All we need to do is set the constructor argument to the location variable:

```
public class Ship {

    private final Location location;
    public Location getLocation() {
        return location;
    }

    public Ship(Location location) {
        this.location = location;
    }

}
```

The full source can be found in the *req01-location* branch of the tdd-java-ch04-ship repository (https://bitbucket.org/vfarcic/tdd-java-ch04-ship/branch/req01-location).

Refactoring

We know that we'll need to instantiate `Ship` for every spec, so we might as well refactor the specification class by adding the `@BeforeMethod` annotation. The code can be the following:

```
@Test
public class ShipSpec {

    private Ship ship;
    private Location location;

    @BeforeMethod
        public void beforeTest() {
        Location location = new Location(
            new Point(21, 13), Direction.NORTH);
        ship = new Ship(location);
    }

    public void whenInstantiatedThenLocationIsSet() {
//        Location location = new Location(
//            new Point(21, 13), Direction.NORTH);
//        Ship ship = new Ship(location);
        assertEquals(ship.getLocation(), location);
    }
}
```

No new behavior has been introduced. We just moved part of the code to the `@BeforeMethod` annotation in order to avoid duplication, which would be produced by the rest of the specifications that we are about to write. Now, every time a test is run, the ship object will be instantiated with `location` as the argument.

Requirement 2

Now that we know where our ship is, let's try to move it. To begin with, we should be able to go both forward and backward.

[Implement commands that move the ship forward and backward (f and b).]

The Location `helper` class already has the `forward` and `backward` methods that implement this functionality:

```
public boolean forward() {
    ...
}
```

Specification

What should happen when, for example, we are facing north and we move the ship forward? Its location on the y axis should decrease. Another example would be that when the ship is facing east, it should increase its x axis location by one.

The first reaction can be to write specifications similar to the following two:

```
public void givenNorthWhenMoveForwardThenYDecreases() {
    ship.moveForward();
    assertEquals(ship.getLocation().getPoint().getY(), 12);
}

public void givenEastWhenMoveForwardThenXIncreases() {
    ship.getLocation().setDirection(Direction.EAST);
    ship.moveForward();
    assertEquals(ship.getLocation().getPoint().getX(), 22);
}
```

We should create at least two more specifications related to cases where a ship is facing south and west.

However, this is not how unit tests should be written. Most people new to UT fall into the trap of specifying the end result that requires the knowledge of the inner workings of methods, classes, and libraries used by the method that is being specified. This approach is problematic on many levels.

When including external code in the unit that is being specified, we should take into account, at least in our case, the fact that the external code is already tested. We know that it is working since we're running all the tests every time any change to the code is done.

Rerun all the tests every time the implementation code changes.

This ensures that there is no unexpected side-effect caused by code changes.

Every time any part of the implementation code changes, all tests should be run. Ideally, tests are fast to execute and can be run by a developer locally. Once code is submitted to the version control, all tests should be run again to ensure that there was no problem due to code merges. This is especially important when more than one developer is working on the code. Continuous Integration tools such as Jenkins, Hudson, Travind, Bamboo and Go-CD should be used to pull the code from the repository, compile it, and run tests.

Another problem with this approach is that if an external code changes, there will be many more specifications to change. Ideally, we should be forced to change only specifications directly related to the unit that will be modified. Searching for all other places where that unit is called from might be very time-consuming and error prone.

A much easier, faster, and better way to write specification for this requirement would be the following:

```
public void whenMoveForwardThenForward() {
    Location expected = location.copy();
    expected.forward();
    ship.moveForward();
    assertEquals(ship.getLocation(), expected);
}
```

Since Location already has the `forward` method, all we'd need to do is to make sure that the proper invocation of that method is performed. We created a new `Location` object called `expected`, invoked the `forward` method, and compared that object with the location of the ship after its `moveForward` method is called.

Note that specifications are not only used to validate the code, but are also used as executable documentation and, most importantly, as a way to think and design. This second attempt specifies more clearly what the intent is behind it. We should create a `moveForward` method inside the `Ship` class and make sure that the `location.forward` is called.

Specification implementation

With such a small and clearly defined specification, it should be fairly easy to write the code that implements it:

```
public boolean moveForward() {
    return location.forward();
}
```

Specification

Now that we have a forward movement specified and implemented, the backward movement should almost be the same:

```
public void whenMoveBackwardThenBackward() {
    Location expected = location.copy();
    expected.backward();
    ship.moveBackward();
    assertEquals(ship.getLocation(), expected);
}
```

Specification implementation

Just like the specification, the backward movement implementation is just as easy:

```
public boolean moveBackward() {
    return location.backward();
}
```

The full source code for this requirement can be found in the `req02-forward-backward` branch of the `tdd-java-ch04-ship` repository (`https://bitbucket.org/vfarcic/tdd-java-ch04-ship/branch/req02-forward-backward`).

Requirement 3

Moving the ship only back and forth, wont, get us far. We should be able to stir by moving it left and right as well.

 Implement commands that turn the ship left and right (l and r).

After implementing the previous requirement, this one should be very easy since it can follow the same logic. The `Location` helper class already contains the `turnLeft` and `turnRight` methods that perform exactly what is required by this requirement. All we need to do is integrate them into the `Ship` class.

Specification

Using the same guidelines as those we have used so far, the specification for turning left can be the following:

```
public void whenTurnLeftThenLeft() {
    Location expected = location.copy();
    expected.turnLeft();
    ship.turnLeft();
    assertEquals(ship.getLocation(), expected);
}
```

Specification implementation

You probably did not have a problem writing the code to pass the previous specification:

```
public void turnLeft() {
    location.turnLeft();
}
```

Specification

Turning right should be almost the same as turning left:

```
public void whenTurnRightThenRight() {
    Location expected = location.copy();
    expected.turnRight();
    ship.turnRight();
    assertEquals(ship.getLocation(), expected);
}
```

Specification implementation

Finally, let's finish this requirement by implementing the specification for turning right:

```
public void turnRight() {
    location.turnRight();
}
```

The full source for this requirement can be found in the `req03-left-right` branch of the `tdd-java-ch04-ship` repository (`https://bitbucket.org/vfarcic/tdd-java-ch04-ship/branch/req03-left-right`).

Requirement 4

Everything we have done so far was fairly easy since there were helper classes that provided all the functionality. This exercise was to learn how to stop attempting to test the end outcome and focus on a unit we're working on. We are building trust; we had to trust the code done by others (the helper classes). Starting from this requirement, you'll have to trust the code you wrote by yourself. We'll continue in the same fashion. We'll write specification, run tests, and see them fail; we'll write implementation, run tests, and see them succeed; finally, we'll refactor if we think the code can be improved. Continue thinking how to test a unit (method) without going deeper into methods or classes that the unit will be invoking.

Now that we have individual commands (forward, backward, left, and right) implemented, it's time to tie it all together. We should create a method that will allow us to pass any number of commands as a single string. Each command should be a character with **f** meaning forward, **b** being backward, **l** for turning left, and **r** for turning right.

 The ship can receive a string with commands (`lrfb` is equivalent to left, right, forward, and backward).

Specification

Let's start with the command argument, that only has the `f` (forward) character:

```
public void whenReceiveCommandsFThenForward() {
    Location expected = location.copy();
    expected.forward();
    ship.receiveCommands("f");
    assertEquals(ship.getLocation(), expected);
}
```

This specification is almost the same as the `whenMoveForwardThenForward` specification except that, this time, we're invoking the `ship.receiveCommands("f")` method.

Specification implementation

We already spoke about the importance of writing the simplest possible code that passes the specification.

Write the simplest code to pass the test. This ensures a cleaner and clearer design and avoids unnecessary features

The idea is that the simpler the implementation, the better and easier it is to maintain the product. The idea adheres to the KISS principle. It states that most systems work best if they are kept simple rather than made complex; therefore, simplicity should be a key goal in design and unnecessary complexity should be avoided.

This is a good opportunity to apply this rule. You might be inclined to write a piece ofcode similar to the following:

```
public void receiveCommands(String commands) {
    if (commands.charAt(0) == 'f') {
        moveForward();
    }
}
```

In this example code, we are verifying whether the first character is f and, if it is, invoking the moveForward method. There are many other variations that we can do. However, if we stick to the simplicity principle, a better solution would be the following:

```
public void receiveCommands(String command) {
    moveForward();
}
```

This is the simplest and shortest possible code that will make the specification pass. Later on, we might end up with something closer to the first version of the code; we might use some kind of a loop or come up with some other solution when things become more complicated. As for now, we are concentrating on one specification at a time and trying to make things simple. We are attempting to clear our mind by focusing only on the task at hand.

For brevity, the rest of the combinations (b, l, and r) are not presented below (continue to implement them by yourself). Instead, we'll jump to the last specification for this requirement.

Specification

Now that we are able to process one command (whatever that the command is), it is time to add the option to send a string of commands. The specification can be the following:

```
public void whenReceiveCommandsThenAllAreExecuted() {
    Location expected = location.copy();
    expected.turnRight();
    expected.forward();
    expected.turnLeft();
    expected.backward();
    ship.receiveCommands("rflb");
    assertEquals(ship.getLocation(), expected);
}
```

This is a bit longer, but is still not an overly complicated specification. We're passing commands `rflb` (right, forward, left, and backward) and expecting that the Location changes accordingly. As before, we're not verifying the end result (seeing whether the if coordinates have changed), but checking whether we are invoking the correct calls to helper methods.

Specification implementation

The end result can be the following:

```
public void receiveCommands(String commands) {
    for (char command : commands.toCharArray()) {
        switch(command) {
            case 'f':
                moveForward();
                break;
            case 'b':
                moveBackward();
                break;
            case 'l':
                turnLeft();
                break;
            case 'r':
                turnRight();
                break;
        }
    }
}
```

If you tried to write specifications and the implementation by yourself and if you followed the simplicity rule, you probably had to refactor your code a couple of times in order to get to the final solution. Simplicity is the key and refactoring is often a welcome necessity. When refactoring, remember that all specifications must be passing all the time.

Refactor only after all the tests have passed.

Benefits: refactoring is safe

If all the implementation code that can be affected has tests and if they are all passing, it is relatively safe to refactor. In most cases, there is no need for new tests; small modifications to existing tests should be enough. The expected outcome of refactoring is to have all the tests passing both before and after the code is modified.

The full source for this requirement can be found in the `req04-commands` branch of the `tdd-java-ch04-ship` repository (`https://bitbucket.org/vfarcic/tdd-java-ch04-ship/branch/req04-commands`).

Requirement 5

Earth is a sphere as any other planet. When Earth is presented as a map, reaching one edge, wraps us to another, for example, when we move east and reach the furthest point in the Pacific Ocean, we are wrapped to the west side of the map and we continue moving towards America. Furthermore, to make the movement easier, we can define the map as a grid. That grid should have length and height expressed as an X and Y axis. That grid should have maximum length (X) and height (Y).

Implement wrapping from one edge of the grid to another.

Specification

The first thing we can do is pass the `Planet` object with the maximum x and y axis coordinates to the `Ship` constructor. Fortunately, `Planet` is one more of the helper classes that are already made (and tested). All we need to do is instantiate it and pass it to the `Ship` constructor:

```
public void whenInstantiatedThenPlanetIsStored() {
    Point max = new Point(50, 50);
    Planet planet = new Planet(max);
```

```
        ship = new Ship(location, planet);
        assertEquals(ship.getPlanet(), planet);
    }
```

We're defining the size of the planet as 50x50 and passing that to the `Planet` class. In turn, that class is afterwards passed to the `Ship` constructor. You might have noticed that the constructor needs an extra argument. In the current code, our constructor requires only `Location`. To implement this specification, it should accept `Planet`, as well.

How would you implement this specification without breaking any of the existing specifications?

Specification implementation

Let's take a bottom-up approach. An assert requires us to have a `planet` getter:

```
private Planet planet;
public Planet getPlanet() {
    return planet;
}
```

Next, the constructor should accept `Planet` as a second argument and assign it to the previously added `planet` variable. The first attempt might be to add it to the existing constructor, but that would break many existing specifications that are using a single argument constructor. This leaves us with only one option: a second constructor:

```
public Ship(Location location) {
    this.location = location;
}
public Ship(Location location, Planet planet) {
    this.location = location;
    this.planet = planet;
}
```

Run all the specifications and confirm that are all successful.

Refactoring

Our specifications forced us to create the second constructor since changing the original one would break the existing tests. However, now that everything is green, we can do some refactoring and get rid of the single argument constructor. The specification class already has the `beforeTest` method that is run before each test. We can move everything, but the assert itself to this method:

```
public class ShipSpec {
    ...
```

```
       private Planet planet;

       @BeforeMethod
       public void beforeTest() {
           Point max = new Point(50, 50);
           location = new Location(new Point(21, 13), Direction.NORTH);
           planet = new Planet(max);
//           ship = new Ship(location);
           ship = new Ship(location, planet);
       }
       public void whenInstantiatedThenPlanetIsStored() {
//           Point max = new Point(50, 50);
//           Planet planet = new Planet(max);
//           ship = new Ship(location, planet);
           assertEquals(ship.getPlanet(), planet);
       }
   }
```

With this change, we effectively removed the usage of the Ship single
argument constructor. By running all specifications, we should confirm
that this change worked.

Now, with a single argument constructor that is not in use any more, we can remove
it from the implementation class, as well:

```
public class Ship {
...
//     public Ship(Location location) {
//         this.location = location;
//     }
       public Ship(Location location, Planet planet) {
           this.location = location;
           this.planet = planet;
       }
...
}
```

By using this approach, all specifications were green all the time. Refactoring did not
change any existing functionality, nothing got broken, and the whole process was
done fast.

Now, let's move into wrapping itself.

Specification

Like in other cases, the helper classes already provide all the functionality that we need. So far, we used the `Location.forward` method without arguments. To implement wrapping, there is the overloaded `Location.forward(Point max)` method that will wrap the location when we reach the end of the grid. With the previous specification, we made sure that `Planet` is passed to the `Ship` class and that it contains `Point max`. Our job is to make sure that `max` is used when moving forward. The specification can be the following:

```
/* The name of this method has been shortened due to line's length
   restrictions. The aim of this test is to check the behavior of
   ship when it is told to overpass the right boundary.
*/
public void overpassEastBoundary() {
    location.setDirection(Direction.EAST);
    location.getPoint().setX(planet.getMax().getX());
    ship.receiveCommands("f");
    assertEquals(location.getX(), 1);
}
```

Specification implementation

By now, you should be getting used to focusing on one unit at a time and to trust that those that were done before are working as expected. This implementation should be no different. We just need to make sure that the maximum coordinates are used when the `location.forward` method is called:

```
    public boolean moveForward() {
//        return location.forward();
        return location.forward(planet.getMax());
    }
```

The same specification and implementation should be done for the backward method. For brevity, it is excluded from this book, but it can be found in the source code.

The full source for this requirement can be found in the `req05-wrap` branch of the `tdd-java-ch04-ship` repository (`https://bitbucket.org/vfarcic/tdd-java-ch04-ship/branch/req05-wrap`).

Requirement 6

We're almost done. This is the last requirement.

Even though most of the Earth is covered in water (approximately 70 percent), there are continents and islands that can be considered as obstacles for our remotely controlled ship. We should have a way to detect whether our next move would hit one of those obstacles. If such a thing happens, the move should be aborted and the ship should stay on the current position and report the obstacle.

> Implement surface detection before each move to a new position.
> If a command encounters a surface, the ship aborts the move, stays
> on the current position, and reports the obstacle.

The specifications and the implementation of this requirement are very similar to those we did previously, and we'll leave that to you.

Here are a few tips that can be useful:

- The `Planet` object has the constructor that accepts a list of obstacles. Each obstacle is an instance of the `Point` class.

- The `Location.foward` and `Location.backward` methods have overloaded versions that accept a list of obstacles. They return `true` if a move was successful and `false` if it failed. Use this Boolean to construct a status report required for the `Ship.receiveCommands` method.

- The `receiveCommands` method should return a string with the status of each command. `0` can represent OK and `X` can be for a failure to move (OOXO = OK, OK, Failure, OK).

The full source for this requirement can be found in the `req06-obstacles` branch of the `tdd-java-ch04-ship` repository (`https://bitbucket.org/vfarcic/tdd-java-ch04-ship/branch/req06-obstacles`).

Summary

In his chapter, we used TestNG as our testing framework of choice. There wasn't much difference when compared to JUnit, simply because we didn't use any of the more advanced features of TestNG (for example, data providers, factories, and so on). With TDD, it is questionable whether we'll ever have a need for those features.

Visit `http://testng.org/`, explore it, and decide for yourself which framework best suits your needs.

The main objective of this chapter was to learn how to focus on one unit at a time. We already had a lot of helper classes and we tried our best to ignore their internal workings. In many cases, we did not write specifications that verified that the end result was correct, but we checked whether the method we were working on invoked the correct method from those helper classes. In the *real world*, you will be working on projects together with other team members, and it is important to learn how to focus on your tasks and trust that what others do works as expected. The same can be said for third-party libraries. It would be too expensive to test all inner processes that can happen when we invoke them. There are other types of tests that will try to cover those possibilities. When working with unit tests, the focus should only be on the unit we're currently working on.

Now that you have a better grasp of how to effectively use unit tests in the context of TDD, it is time to dive into some other advantages that test-driven development provides. Specifically, we'll explore how to better design our applications.

5
Design – If It's Not Testable, It's Not Designed Well

"Simplicity is the ultimate sophistication."

Leonardo da Vinci

In the past, the software industry was focused on developing software at high speed, with nothing in mind but cost and time. Quality was a secondary goal, with the fake feeling that customers were not interested in it.

Nowadays, with the increasing connectivity of all kinds of platforms and devices, quality becomes a first-class citizen in customers' requirements. Good applications offer a good service with a reasonable response-time, without being affected by a multitude of concurrent requests from many users.

Good applications in terms of quality are those that have been well designed. A good design means scalability, security, maintainability, and many other desired attributes.

In this chapter, we will explore how TDD leads developers to good design and best practices by implementing the same application using both the traditional and TDD approaches.

The following topics will be covered in this chapter:

- Why should we care about design?
- Design considerations
- The traditional development process
- The TDD approach
- Hamcrest

Why should we care about design?

In the coding world, whether you are an expert or a beginner, there are some scenarios where code seems to be weird. You can't avoid a feeling that something is wrong with the code when reading it. You even occasionally wonder why the previous programmer implemented a specific method or a class in such a bad manner. This is because the same functionality can be implemented in a vast number of different ways, each of them being unique. With this big number of possibilities, which is the best one? The answer is that all of them are valid as they all achieve the goal. However, it is true that some considerations should be taken into account while finding better solutions. This is where design becomes important.

Design principles

The TDD philosophy encourages programmers to follow some principles and good practices that make code cleaner and more readable. As a result, our code becomes easy to understand and safe to modify in the future. Let's take a look at some of the basic software design principles.

You Ain't Gonna Need It

YAGNI is the acronym for the *You Ain't Gonna Need It* principle. It aims to erase all unnecessary code and focuses on the current functionalities, not the future ones. The less code you have, the less code you're going to maintain and the less probability that bugs are introduced.

For more information on YAGNI, visit *Martin Fowler's* article available at `http://martinfowler.com/bliki/Yagni.html`.

Don't Repeat Yourself

The idea behind the **Don't Repeat Yourself (DRY)** principle is to reuse the code you previously wrote instead of repeating it. The benefits are less code to maintain and the use of code that you know that already works, which is a great thing. It helps you to discover new abstraction levels inside your code.

For additional information, visit `http://en.wikipedia.org/wiki/Don%27t_repeat_yourself`.

Keep It Simple, Stupid

This principle has the confusing acronym of KISS and states that things perform their function better if they are kept simple rather than complicated. It was coined by Kelly Johnson.

To read about the story behind this principle, visit `http://en.wikipedia.org/wiki/KISS_principle`.

Occam's Razor

Although Occam's Razor is not a software engineering principle but a philosophical one, it is still applicable to what we do, and is very similar to the previous principle with the main derived statement being as follows:

> *"When you have two competing solutions to the same problem, the simpler one is the better."*

> *William of Ockham*

For more information on Occam's razor, visit `http://en.wikipedia.org/wiki/Occam%27s_razor`.

SOLID

The word **SOLID** is an acronym invented by *Robert C. Martin* for the five basic principles of object-oriented programming. By following these five principles, a developer is more likely to create a great, durable, and maintainable application:

- **Single Responsibility Principle**: A class should have only a single reason to change.

- **Open-Closed Principle**: A class should be open for extension and closed for modification. This is attributed to *Bertrand Meyer*.

- **Liskov Substitution Principle**: This was created by *Barbara Liskov,* and she says *a class should be replaceable by others that extend that class.*

- **Interface Segregation Principle**: A few specific interfaces are preferable than one general-purpose interface.

- **Dependency Inversion Principle**: A class should depend on abstraction instead of implementation. This means that class dependencies must be focused on what is done and forget about how it is done.

For further information on SOLID or other related principles, visit `http://butunclebob.com/ArticleS.UncleBob.PrinciplesOfOod`.

The first four principles are part of the core of TDD thinking, since they aim to simplify the code we write. The last one is focused on classes construction and dependency relationships in the application assembly process.

All of these principles are applicable and desirable in both test and non-test driven development, because, apart from other benefits, they make our code more maintainable. The proper practical application of them is worth a whole book by itself. While we won't have time to go deep into it, we encourage you to investigate further.

In this chapter, we will see how TDD induces developers to put some of these principles in to practice effortlessly. We will implement a small but yet fully functional version of the famous game **Connect4** with both TDD and non-TDD approach. Note that repetitive parts, such as Gradle project creation and so on, are omitted, as they are not considered relevant for the purpose of this chapter.

Connect4

Connect4 is a popular, very easy-to-play board game. The rules are limited and simple.

Connect4 is a two-player connection game, in which the players first choose a color and then take turns dropping colored discs from the top into a seven-column, six-row, vertically suspended grid. The pieces fall straight down, occupying the next available space within the column. The objective of the game is to connect four of one's own discs of the same color next to each other vertically, horizontally, or diagonally, before your opponent connects four of theirs.

For further information on the game, visit Wikipedia (`http://en.wikipedia.org/wiki/Connect_Four`).

Requirements

In order to code the two implementations of Connect4, the game rules are transcribed below in the form of requirements. These requirements are the starting point for both the developments. We will go through the code with some explanations and compare both implementations at the end:

1. The board is composed of seven columns and six rows, all positions are emptys.

2. Players introduce discs on the top of the columns. The introduced disc drops down the board if the column is empty. Future discs introduced in the same column will stack over the previous ones.

3. It is a two-person game, so there is one color for each player. One player uses red ('R') and the other one uses green ('G'). Players alternate turns, inserting one disc every time.

4. We want feedback when either an event or an error occurs within the game. The output shows the status of the board after every move.

5. When no more discs can be inserted, the game finishes, and it is considered a draw.

6. If a player inserts a disc and connects more than three discs of his color in a straight vertical line, then that player wins.

7. The same happens in a horizontal line direction.

8. The same happens in a diagonal line direction.

Test the last implementation of Connect4

This is the traditional approach, focusing on problem-solving code rather than tests. Some people and companies forget about the value of automated testing. and rely on users in what are called **user acceptance tests**.

This kind of user acceptance test consists of recreating real-world scenarios in a controlled environment, ideally identical to production. Some users perform a lot of different tasks to verify the correctness of the application. If any of these actions fail, then the code is not accepted as it is breaking some functionality or it is not working as expected.

Moreover, a great number of these companies also use unit testing as a way to perform early regression checks. These unit tests are programmed after the development process and they try to cover as much code as possible. Last of all, code coverage analysis is executed to get a trace of what is actually covered by those unit tests; the bigger the code coverage, the better the quality delivered.

Let's implement the Connect4 game using this approach. The relevant code for each of the identified requirements is presented below. This code isn't written incrementally, so some code snippets might contain a few code lines nonrelated to the mentioned requirement.

Requirement 1

Let us start with the first requirement.

[The board is composed of seven horizontal and six vertical empty positions.]

The implementation of this requirement is pretty straightforward. We just need the representation of an empty position and the data structure to hold the game. Note that the colors used by players are also defined:

```java
public class Connect4 {
    public enum Color {
        RED('R'), GREEN('G'), EMPTY(' ');

        private final char value;

        Color(char value) { this.value = value; }

        @Override
        public String toString() {
            return String.valueOf(value);
        }
    }

    public static final int COLUMNS = 7;

    public static final int ROWS = 6;

    private Color[][] board = new Color[COLUMNS][ROWS];

    public Connect4() {
        for (Color[] column : board) {
            Arrays.fill(column, Color.EMPTY);
        }
    }
}
```

Requirement 2

The second requirement starts drawing the logic of the game.

 Players introduce discs on the top of the columns. The introduced disc drops down the board if the column is empty. Future discs introduced in the same column will stack over the previous ones.

In this part, board bounds become relevant. We need to mark what positions are already taken, using `Color.RED` to indicate them. Finally, the first private method is created. It is a helper method that calculates the number of discs introduced in a given column:

```java
public void putDisc(int column) {
    if (column > 0 && column <= COLUMNS) {
        int numOfDiscs =
        getNumberOfDiscsInColumn(column - 1);
        if (numOfDiscs < ROWS) {
            board[column - 1][numOfDiscs] =
            Color.RED;
        }
    }
}

private int getNumberOfDiscsInColumn(int column) {
    if (column >= 0 && column < COLUMNS) {
        int row;
        for (row = 0; row < ROWS; row++) {
            if (Color.EMPTY == board[column][row]) {
                return row;
            }
        }
        return row;
    }
    return -1;
}
```

Requirement 3

More game logic is introduced with this requirement.

 It is a two-person game, so there is one colour for each player. One player uses red ('R') and the other one uses green ('G'). Players alternate turns, inserting one disc every time.

We need to save the current player in order to determine which player is playing this turn. We also need a function to switch the players in order to recreate the logic of turns. Some lines of code become relevant in the `putDisc` function. Specifically, the board position assignment is made using the current player, and it is switched afterevery move, as the game rules say:

```
...
private Color currentPlayer = Color.RED;

private void switchPlayer() {
    if (Color.RED == currentPlayer)
        currentPlayer = Color.GREEN;
    } else {
        currentPlayer = Color.RED;
    }
}

public void putDisc(int column) {
    if (column > 0 && column <= COLUMNS) {
        int numOfDiscs =
        getNumberOfDiscsInColumn(column - 1);
        if (numOfDiscs < ROWS) {
            board[column - 1][numOfDiscs] =
             currentPlayer;
            switchPlayer();
        }
    }
}
...
```

Requirement 4

A few outputs should be added in order to let the players know the current status of the game.

 We want a feedback when either an event or an error occurs within the game. The output shows the status of the board after every move.

No output channel is specified. To make it easier, we decided to use the system standard output to print an event when it occurs. A few lines have been added on every action to let the user know about the status of the game:

```
...
private static final String DELIMITER = "|";

private void switchPlayer() {
    if (Color.RED == currentPlayer) {
        currentPlayer = Color.GREEN;
    } else {
        currentPlayer = Color.RED;
    }
    System.out.println("Current turn: " +
        currentPlayer);
}

public void printBoard() {
    for (int row = ROWS - 1; row >= 0; --row) {
        StringJoiner stringJoiner =
            new StringJoiner(DELIMITER,
                    DELIMITER,
                    DELIMITER);
        for (int col = 0; col < COLUMNS; ++col) {
            stringJoiner
            .add(board[col][row].toString());
        }
        System.out.println(
        stringJoiner.toString());
    }
}

public void putDisc(int column) {
    if (column > 0 && column <= COLUMNS) {
```

```
        int numOfDiscs =
        getNumberOfDiscsInColumn(column - 1);
        if (numOfDiscs < ROWS) {
            board[column - 1][numOfDiscs] =
            currentPlayer;
            printBoard();
            switchPlayer();
        } else {
            System.out.println(numOfDiscs);
            System.out.println("There's no room " +
              "for a new disc in this column");
            printBoard();
        }
    } else {
        System.out.println("Column out of bounds");
        printBoard();
    }
}
...
```

Requirement 5

The first game has a finished condition.

 [When no more discs can be inserted, the game finishes and it is considered a draw.]

The following code shows one of the possible implementations:

```
...
public boolean isFinished() {
    int numOfDiscs = 0;
    for (int col = 0; col < COLUMNS; ++col) {
        numOfDiscs +=
        getNumberOfDiscsInColumn(col);
    }
    if (numOfDiscs >= COLUMNS * ROWS) {
        System.out.println("It's a draw");
        return true;
    }
    return false;
}
...
```

Requirement 6

The first win condition.

 If a player inserts a disc and connects more than three discs of his colour in a straight vertical line, then that player wins.

The `checkWinCondition` private method implements this rule by scanning whether or not the last move is a winning one:

```
...
private Color winner;

public static final int DISCS_FOR_WIN = 4;

public void putDisc(int column) {
        ...
        if (numOfDiscs < ROWS) {
            board[column - 1][numOfDiscs] =
            currentPlayer;
            printBoard();
            checkWinCondition(column - 1,
            numOfDiscs);
            switchPlayer();
        ...
}

private void checkWinCondition(int col, int row) {
    Pattern winPattern =
        Pattern.compile(".*" + currentPlayer +
        "{" + DISCS_FOR_WIN + "}.*");

    // Vertical check
    StringJoiner stringJoiner =
        new StringJoiner("");
    for (int auxRow = 0; auxRow < ROWS; ++auxRow) {
        stringJoiner
        .add(board[col][auxRow].toString());
    }
    if (winPattern.matcher(stringJoiner.toString())
            .matches()) {
        winner = currentPlayer;
```

```
            System.out.println(currentPlayer +
            " wins");
        }
    }

    public boolean isFinished() {
        if (winner != null) return true;
        ...
    }
    ...
```

Requirement 7

This is the same win condition, but in a different direction.

 If a player inserts a disc and connects more than three discs of his color in a straight horizontal line, then that player wins.

A few lines to implement this rule are as follows:

```
    ...
    private void checkWinCondition(int col, int row) {
        ...
        // Horizontal check
        stringJoiner = new StringJoiner("");
        for (int column = 0; column < COLUMNS;
                ++column) {
            stringJoiner
            .add(board[column][row].toString());
        }
        if (winPattern.matcher(stringJoiner.toString())
            .matches()) {
            winner = currentPlayer;
            System.out.println(currentPlayer +
              " wins");
            return;
        }
        ...
    }
    ...
```

Requirement 8

The last requirement is the last win condition. It is pretty similar to the last two; in this case, in diagonal direction.

 If a player inserts a disc and connects more than three discs of his color in a straight diagonal line, then that player wins.

This is a possible implementation for this last requirement. The code is very similar to the other win conditions because the same statement must be fulfilled:

```
...
private void checkWinCondition(int col, int row) {
    ...
    // Diagonal checks
    int startOffset = Math.min(col, row);
    int column = col - startOffset,
        auxRow = row - startOffset;
    stringJoiner = new StringJoiner("");
    do {
        stringJoiner
            .add(board[column++][auxRow++].toString());
    } while (column < COLUMNS && auxRow < ROWS);

     if (winPattern.matcher(stringJoiner.toString())
         .matches()) {
        winner = currentPlayer;
        System.out.println(currentPlayer +
        " wins");
        return;
    }

    startOffset = Math.min(col, ROWS - 1 - row);
    column = col - startOffset;
    auxRow = row + startOffset;
    stringJoiner = new StringJoiner("");
    do {
        stringJoiner
            .add(board[column++][auxRow--].toString());
    } while (column < COLUMNS && auxRow >= 0);

    if (winPattern.matcher(stringJoiner.toString())
        .matches()) {
```

```
        winner = currentPlayer;
        System.out.println(currentPlayer +
        " wins");
    }
}
...
```

What we have got is a class with one constructor, three `public` methods, and three `private` methods. The logic of the application is distributed among all methods. The biggest flaw here is that this class is very difficult to maintain. The crucial methods, such as `checkWinCondition`, are not-trivial with potential for bug entries in future modifications.

If you want to take a look at the full code, you can find it in the `https://bitbucket.org/vfarcic/tdd-java-ch05-design.git` repository.

We made this small example to demonstrate the common problems with this approach. Topics such as the SOLID principle requires a bigger project to become more illustrative.

In large projects with hundreds of classes, the problems bring hours wasted in a sort of surgical development. Developers spend major part of their time investigating tricky code and understanding how it works, instead of creating new features.

The TDD implementation of Connect4

At this time, we know how TDD works: writing tests before, implementation after tests, and refactoring later on. We are going to pass through that process and only show the final result for each requirement. It is left to you to figure out the iterative red-green-refactor process. Let's make this more interesting, if possible, by using a Hamcrest framework in our tests.

Hamcrest

As described in *Chapter 2, Tools, Frameworks, and Environment*, Hamcrest improves our tests readability. It turns assertions more semantic and comprehensive at the time that complexity is reduced by using matchers. When a test fails, the error shown becomes more expressive by interpreting the matchers used in the assertion. A message could also be added by the developer.

The `Hamcrest` library is full of different matchers for different object types and collections. Let's start coding and get a taste of it.

Requirement 1

We will start with the first requirement.

 The board is composed by seven horizontal and six vertical empty positions.

There is no big challenge with this requirement. The board bounds are specified, but there's no described behavior in it; just the consideration of an empty board when the game starts. That means zero discs when the game begins. However, this requirement must be taken into account later on.

Tests

This is how the test class looks for this requirement. There's a method to initialize the tested class in order to use a completely fresh object in each test. There's also the first test to verify that there's no disc when we start the game, meaning that all board positions are empty:

```
public class Connect4TDDSpec {

    private Connect4TDD tested;

    @Before
    public void beforeEachTest() {
        tested = new Connect4TDD();
    }

    @Test
    public void whenTheGameIsStartedTheBoardIsEmpty() {
        assertThat(tested.getNumberOfDiscs(), is(0));
    }

}
```

Code

This is the TDD implementation of the previous specification. Observe the simplicity of the given solution for this first requirement; a simple method returning the result in a single line:

```java
public class Connect4TDD {

    public int getNumberOfDiscs() {
        return 0;
    }

}
```

Requirement 2

This is the implementation of the second requirement.

 Players introduce discs on the top of the columns. An introduced disc drops down the board if the column is empty. Future discs introduced in the same column will stack over the previous ones.

- We can split this requirement into the following tests:
- When a disc is inserted into an empty column, its position is 0
- When a second disc is inserted into the same column, its position is 1
- When a disc is inserted into the board, the total number of discs increases
- When a disc is put outside the boundaries, a Runtime Exception is thrown
- When a disc is inserted in to a column and there's no room available for it, then a Runtime Exception is thrown

Also, these other tests are derived from the first requirement. They are related to the board limits or board behaviour.

Tests

The Java implementation of the afore mentioned tests is as follows:

```java
@Test
public void
whenDiscOutsideBoardThenRuntimeException() {
    int column = -1;
    exception.expect(RuntimeException.class);
    exception.expectMessage("Invalid column " +
```

```
        column);
    tested.putDiscInColumn(column);
}

@Test
public void
whenFirstDiscInsertedInColumnThenPositionIsZero() {
    int column = 1;
    assertThat(tested.putDiscInColumn(column),
            is(0));
}

@Test
public void
whenSecondDiscInsertedInColumnThenPositionIsOne() {
        int column = 1;
        tested.putDiscInColumn(column);
        assertThat(tested.putDiscInColumn(column),
        is(1));
    }

@Test
public void
whenDiscInsertedThenNumberOfDiscsIncreases() {
    int column = 1;
    tested.putDiscInColumn(column);
    assertThat(tested.getNumberOfDiscs(), is(1));
}

@Test
public void
whenNoMoreRoomInColumnThenRuntimeException() {
    int column = 1;
    int maxDiscsInColumn = 6; // the number of rows
    for (int times = 0;
        times < maxDiscsInColumn;
        ++times) {
        tested.putDiscInColumn(column);
    }
    exception.expect(RuntimeException.class);
    exception
        .expectMessage("No more room in column " +
            column);
    tested.putDiscInColumn(column);
}
```

Code

This is the necessary code to satisfy the tests:

```java
private static final int ROWS = 6;

private static final int COLUMNS = 7;

private static final String EMPTY = " ";

private String[][] board =
    new String[ROWS][COLUMNS];

public Connect4TDD() {
    for (String[] row : board)
        Arrays.fill(row, EMPTY);
}

public int getNumberOfDiscs() {
    return IntStream.range(0, COLUMNS)
            .map(this::getNumberOfDiscsInColumn).sum();
}

private int getNumberOfDiscsInColumn(int column) {
    return (int) IntStream.range(0, ROWS)
            .filter(row -> !EMPTY
            .equals(board[row][column]))
            .count();
}

public int putDiscInColumn(int column) {
    checkColumn(column);
    int row = getNumberOfDiscsInColumn(column);
    checkPositionToInsert(row, column);
    board[row][column] = "X";
    return row;
}

private void checkColumn(int column) {
    if (column < 0 || column >= COLUMNS)
        throw new RuntimeException(
        "Invalid column " + column);
}

private void
```

```
checkPositionToInsert(int row, int column) {
    if (row == ROWS)
        throw new RuntimeException(
          "No more room in column " + column);
}
```

Requirement 3

The third requirement specifies the game logic.

[It is a two-person game, so there is one colour for each player. One player uses red ('R') and the other one uses green ('G'). Players alternate turns, inserting one disc every time.]

Tests

These tests cover the verification of the new functionality. For the sake of simplicity, the red player will always start the game:

```
@Test
public void
whenFirstPlayerPlaysThenDiscColorIsRed() {
    assertThat(tested.getCurrentPlayer(), is("R"));
}

@Test
public void
whenSecondPlayerPlaysThenDiscColorIsRed() {
    int column = 1;
    tested.putDiscInColumn(column);
    assertThat(tested.getCurrentPlayer(), is("G"));
}
```

Code

A couple of methods need to be created to cover this functionality.
The switchPlayer method is called before returning the row in the
putDiscInColumn method:

```
private static final String RED = "R";

private static final String GREEN = "G";
```

```
    private String currentPlayer = RED;

    public Connect4TDD() {
        for (String[] row : board)
            Arrays.fill(row, EMPTY);
    }

    public String getCurrentPlayer() {
        return currentPlayer;
    }

    private void switchPlayer() {
        if (RED.equals(currentPlayer))
            currentPlayer = GREEN;
        else currentPlayer = RED;
    }

    public int putDiscInColumn(int column) {
        ...
        switchPlayer();
        return row;
    }
```

Requirement 4

Next, we should let the player know the status of the game.

 We want feedback when either an event or an error occurs within the game. The output shows the status of the board on every move.

Tests

As we are throwing exceptions when an error occurs, this is already covered, so we only need to implement these two tests. Furthermore, for the sake of testability, we need to introduce a parameter within the constructor. By introducing this parameter, the output becomes easier to test:

```
    private OutputStream output;

    @Before
    public void beforeEachTest() {
        output = new ByteArrayOutputStream();
```

```
    tested = new Connect4TDD(
        new PrintStream(output));
}

@Test
public void
whenAskedForCurrentPlayerTheOutputNotice() {
    tested.getCurrentPlayer();
    assertThat(output.toString(),
        containsString("Player R turn"));
}

@Test
public void
whenADiscIsIntroducedTheBoardIsPrinted() {
    int column = 1;
    tested.putDiscInColumn(column);
    assertThat(output.toString(),
        containsString("| |R| | | | | |"));
}
```

Code

One possible implementation is to pass the above tests. As you can see, the class
constructor now has one parameter. This parameter is used in several methods to
print the event or action description:

```
private static final String DELIMITER = "|";

public Connect4TDD(PrintStream out) {
    outputChannel = out;
    for (String[] row : board)
        Arrays.fill(row, EMPTY);
}

public String getCurrentPlayer() {
    outputChannel.printf("Player %s turn%n",
        currentPlayer);
    return currentPlayer;
}

private void printBoard() {
    for (int row = ROWS - 1; row >= 0; row--) {
        StringJoiner stringJoiner =
```

```
            new StringJoiner(DELIMITER,
                            DELIMITER,
                            DELIMITER);
        Stream.of(board[row])
        .forEachOrdered(stringJoiner::add);
        outputChannel
        .println(stringJoiner.toString());
    }
}

public int putDiscInColumn(int column) {
    ...
    printBoard();
    switchPlayer();
    return row;
}
```

Requirement 5

This requirement tells the system whether the game is finished.

 When no more discs can be inserted, the game finishes and it is considered a draw.

Tests

There are two conditions to test. The first condition is that new games must be unfinished; the second condition is that full board games must be finished:

```
@Test
public void whenTheGameStartsItIsNotFinished() {
    assertFalse("The game must not be finished",
        tested.isFinished());
}

@Test
public void
whenNoDiscCanBeIntroducedTheGamesIsFinished() {
    for (int row = 0; row < 6; row++)
        for (int column = 0; column < 7; column++)
            tested.putDiscInColumn(column);
    assertTrue("The game must be finished",
        tested.isFinished());
}
```

Code

An easy and simple solution to these two tests is as follows:

```
public boolean isFinished() {
    return getNumberOfDiscs() == ROWS * COLUMNS;
}
```

Requirement 6

This is the first win condition requirement.

[If a player inserts a disc and connects more than three discs of his color in a straight vertical line, then that player wins.]

Tests

In fact, this requires one single check. If the current inserted disc connects other three discs in a vertical line, the current player wins the game:

```
@Test
public void
when4VerticalDiscsAreConnectedThenPlayerWins() {
    for (int row = 0; row < 3; row++) {
        tested.putDiscInColumn(1); // R
        tested.putDiscInColumn(2); // G
    }
    assertThat(tested.getWinner(),
        isEmptyString());
    tested.putDiscInColumn(1); // R
    assertThat(tested.getWinner(), is("R"));
}
```

Code

There are a couple of changes to the putDiscInColumn method. Also, a new method called checkWinner has been created:

```
private static final int DISCS_TO_WIN = 4;

private String winner = "";
```

```
private void checkWinner(int row, int column) {
    if (winner.isEmpty()) {
        String colour = board[row][column];
        Pattern winPattern =
        Pattern.compile(".*" + colour + "{" +
            DISCS_TO_WIN + "}.*");

        String vertical = IntStream.range(0, ROWS)
                .mapToObj(r -> board[r][column])
                .reduce(String::concat).get();
        if (winPattern.matcher(vertical).matches())
            winner = colour;
    }
}
```

Requirement 7

This is the second win condition, which is pretty similar to the previous one.

 If a player inserts a disc and connects more than three discs of his color in a straight horizontal line, then that player wins.

Tests

This time, we are trying to win the game by inserting discs into adjacent columns:

```
@Test
public void
when4HorizontalDiscsAreConnectedThenPlayerWins() {
    int column;
    for (column = 0; column < 3; column++) {
        tested.putDiscInColumn(column); // R
        tested.putDiscInColumn(column); // G
    }
    assertThat(tested.getWinner(),
        isEmptyString());
    tested.putDiscInColumn(column); // R
    assertThat(tested.getWinner(), is("R"));
}
```

Code

The code to pass this test is put into the `checkWinners` method:

```
if (winner.isEmpty()) {
    String horizontal =
        Stream
        .of(board[row])
        .reduce(String::concat).get();
    if (winPattern.matcher(horizontal)
        .matches())
        winner = colour;
}
```

Requirement 8

The last requirement is the last win condition.

 If a player inserts a disc and connects more than three discs of his colour in a straight diagonal line, then that player wins.

Tests

We need to perform valid game movements to achieve the condition. In this case, we need to test both diagonals across the board: from top-right to bottom-left and from bottom-right to top-left. The following tests use a list of columns to recreate a full game to reproduce the scenario under test:

```
@Test
public void
when4Diagonal1DiscsAreConnectedThenThatPlayerWins()
{
    int[] gameplay =
        new int[] {1, 2, 2, 3, 4, 3, 3, 4, 4, 5, 4};
    for (int column : gameplay) {
        tested.putDiscInColumn(column);
    }
    assertThat(tested.getWinner(), is("R"));
}

@Test
public void
when4Diagonal2DiscsAreConnectedThenThatPlayerWins()
{
    int[] gameplay =
        new int[] {3, 4, 2, 3, 2, 2, 1, 1, 1, 1};
```

```
    for (int column : gameplay) {
        tested.putDiscInColumn(column);
    }
    assertThat(tested.getWinner(), is("G"));
}
```

Code

Again, the `checkWinner` method needs to be modified, adding new board verifications:

```
if (winner.isEmpty()) {
    int startOffset = Math.min(column, row);
    int myColumn = column - startOffset,
        myRow = row - startOffset;
    StringJoiner stringJoiner =
    new StringJoiner("");
    do {
        stringJoiner
        .add(board[myRow++][myColumn++]);
    } while (myColumn < COLUMNS &&
            myRow < ROWS);
    if (winPattern
    .matcher(stringJoiner.toString())
        .matches())
        winner = currentPlayer;
}

if (winner.isEmpty()) {
    int startOffset =
    Math.min(column, ROWS - 1 - row);
    int myColumn = column - startOffset,
        myRow = row + startOffset;
    StringJoiner stringJoiner =
    new StringJoiner("");
    do {
        stringJoiner
        .add(board[myRow--][myColumn++]);
    } while (myColumn < COLUMNS &&
            myRow >= 0);
    if (winPattern
        .matcher(stringJoiner.toString())
        .matches())
        winner = currentPlayer;
}
```

Using TDD, we got a class with a constructor, five public methods, and six private methods. In general, all methods look pretty simple and easy to understand. In this approach, we also get a big method to check winner conditions: `checkWinner`. The advantage is that this approach has useful tests to guarantee that future modifications do not alter the behavior of the method. Code coverage wasn't the goal, but we got a high percentage.

Additionally, for testing purposes, we refactored the constructor of the class to accept the output channel as a parameter. If we need to modify the way the game status is printed, it will be easier that way than replacing all the uses in the traditional approach. Hence, it is more extensible.

In large projects, when you detect that a great number of tests must be created for a single class, this enables you to split this class following the **Single Responsibility Principle**. As the output printing was delegated to an external class passed in a parameter in initialization, a more elegant solution would be to create a class with high-level printing methods. This is just to keep the printing logic separated from the game logic. These are examples of benefits of good design using TDD.

Connect4 > com.packtpublishing.tddjava.ch05connect4 > Connect4TDD

Connect4TDD

Element	Missed Instructions	Cov.	Missed Branches	Cov.	Missed	Cxty	Missed	Lines	Missed	Methods
checkWinner(int, int)		100%		100%	0	13	0	29	0	1
Connect4TDD(PrintStream)		100%		100%	0	2	0	8	0	1
printBoard()		100%		100%	0	2	0	5	0	1
putDiscInColumn(int)		100%		n/a	0	1	0	8	0	1
checkColumn(int)		100%		75%	1	3	0	3	0	1
checkPositionToInsert(int, int)		100%		100%	0	2	0	3	0	1
getCurrentPlayer()		100%		n/a	0	1	0	2	0	1
switchPlayer()		100%		100%	0	2	0	4	0	1
getNumberOfDiscsInColumn(int)		100%		n/a	0	1	0	3	0	1
getNumberOfDiscs()		100%		n/a	0	1	0	2	0	1
isFinished()		100%		100%	0	2	0	1	0	1
getWinner()		100%		n/a	0	1	0	1	0	1
Total	0 of 356	100%	1 of 38	97%	1	31	0	69	0	12

The code of this approach is available at
`https://bitbucket.org/vfarcic/tdd-java-ch05-design.git`.

Summary

In this chapter, we briefly talked about software design and a few basic design principles. We implemented a fully-functional version of the board game Connect4 using two approaches: traditional and test-driven development.

We analyzed both solutions in terms of pros and cons, and used a Hamcrest framework to empower our tests.

Finally, we concluded that good design and good practices can be performed by both approaches, but TDD leads developers to the better way.

For further information about the topics that this chapter covers, refer to two highly recommended books written by *Robert C. Martin: Clean Code: A Handbook of Agile Software Craftsmanship* and *Agile Software Development: Principles, Patterns, and Practices.*

6
Mocking – Removing External Dependencies

"Talk is cheap. Show me the code."

- *Linus Torvalds*

TDD is about speed. We want to quickly demonstrate whether some idea, concept, or implementation, is valid or not. Further on, we want to run all tests fast. A major bottleneck to this speed is external dependencies. Setting up DB data required by tests can be time-consuming. The execution of tests that verify code that uses third-party API can be slow. Most importantly, writing tests that satisfy all external dependencies can become too complicated to be worthwhile. Mocking both external and internal dependencies helps us solve these problems.

We'll build on what we did in *Chapter 3, Red-Green-Refactor - From Failure Through Success Until Perfection*. We'll extend Tic-Tac-Toe to use MongoDB as data storage. None of our unit tests will actually use MongoDB since all communications will be mocked. At the end, we'll create an integration test that will verify that our code and MongoDB are indeed integrated.

The following topics will be covered in this chapter:

- Mocking
- Mockito
- Tic-Tac-Toe v2 requirements
- Developing Tic-Tac-Toe v2
- Integration tests

Mocking

Everyone who did any of the applications more complicated than "Hello World," knows that Java code is full of dependencies. There can be classes and methods written by other members of the team, third-party libraries, or external systems that we communicate with. Even libraries found inside JDK are dependencies. We might have a business layer that communicates with data access layer that, in turn, uses database drivers to fetch data. When working with unit tests, we take dependencies even further and often consider all public and protected methods (even those inside the class we are working on) as dependencies that should be isolated.

When doing TDD on unit tests level, creating specifications that contemplate all those dependencies can be so complex that the tests themselves would become bottlenecks. Their development time can increase so much that the benefits gained with TDD quickly become overshadowed by the ever-increasing cost. More importantly, those same dependencies tend to create such complex tests that they contain more bugs than the implementation itself.

The idea of unit testing (especially when tied to TDD) is to write specifications that validate whether the code of a single unit works regardless of dependencies. When dependencies are internal, they are already tested, and we know that they do what we expect them to do. On the other hand, external dependencies require trust. We must believe that they work correctly. Even if we don't, the task work of performing deep testing of, let's say, the JDK `java.nio` classes is too big for most of us. Besides, those potential problems will surface when we run functional and integration tests.

While focused on units, we must try to remove all dependencies that a unit might use. Removal of those dependencies is accomplished through a combination of design and mocking.

Using mocks

Benefits include reduced code dependency and faster tests execution.

Mocks are prerequisites for the fast execution of tests and the ability to concentrate on a single unit of functionality. By mocking dependencies external to the method that is being tested, the developer is able to focus on the task at hand without spending time setting them up. In a case of bigger or multiple teams working together, those dependencies might not even be developed. Also, execution of tests without mocks tends to be slow. Good candidates for mocks are databases, other products, services, and so on.

Before we go deeper into mocks, let us go through reasons why one would employ them in the first place.

Why mocks?

The following list represents some of the reasons why we employ mock objects:

- The object generates nondeterministic results. For example, `java.util.Date()` provides a different result every time we instantiate it. We cannot test that its result is as expected:

  ```
  java.util.Date date = new java.util.Date();
  date.getTime(); // What is
  the result this method returns?
  ```

- The object does not yet exist. For example, we might create an interface and test against it. The object that implements that interface might not have been written at the time we test code that uses that interface.

- The object is slow and requires time to process. The most common example would be databases. We might have a code that retrieves all records and generates a report. This operation can last minutes, hours, or, in some cases, even days.

The above mentioned reasons for mock objects apply to any type of testing. However, in the case of unit tests and, especially, in the context of TDD, there is one more reason, perhaps more important than others. Mocking allows us to isolate all dependencies used by a the method we are currently working on. This empowers us to concentrate on a single unit and ignore the inner workings of the code that the unit invokes.

Terminology

Terminology can be a bit confusing, especially since different people use different names for the same thing. To make things even more complicated, mocking frameworks tend not to be consistent when naming their methods.

Before we proceed, let us briefly go through terminology.

Test doubles is a generic name for all of the following types:

- Dummy object's purpose is to act as a substitute for a `real` method argument
- Test Stub can be used to replace a real object with a test-specific object that feeds the desired indirect inputs into the system under test
- Test spy captures the indirect output calls made to another component by the **system under test (SUT)** for later verification by the test

- Mock Object replaces an object the system under test (SUT) depends on, with a test-specific object that verifies that it is being used correctly by the SUT

- Fake object replaces a component that the system under test (SUT) depends on with a much lighter-weight implementation

If you are confused, it might help you to know that you are not the only one. Things are even more complicated than this, since there is no clear agreement, nor a naming standard, between frameworks or authors. Terminology is confusing and inconsistent, and the terms mentioned above are by no means accepted by everyone.

To simplify things, throughout this book we'll use the same naming used by Mockito (our framework of choice). This way, methods that you'll be using will correspond with the terminology that you'll be reading further on. We'll continue using mocking as a general term for what others might call *test doubles*. Furthermore, we'll use a mock or spy term to refer to Mockito methods.

Mock objects

Mock objects simulate the behavior of real (often complex) objects. They allow us to create an object that will replace the *real* one used in the implementation code. A mocked object will expect a defined method with defined arguments to return the expected result. It knows in advance what is supposed to happen and how we expect it to react.

Let's take a look at one simple example:

```
TicTacToeCollection collection =
    mock(TicTacToeCollection.class);

assertThat(collection.drop()).isFalse();

doReturn(true).when(collection).drop();

assertThat(collection.drop()).isTrue();
```

First, we defined `collection` to be a mock of `TicTacToeCollection`. At this moment, all methods from this mocked object are *fake* and, in the case of Mockito, return default values. This is confirmed in the second line, where we assert that the `drop` method returns `false`. Further on, we specify that our mocked object collection should return `true` when the `drop` method is invoked. Finally, we assert that the `drop` method returns `true`.

We created a mock object that returns default values and, for one of its methods, defined what should be the return value. At no point was a *real* object used.

Later on, we'll work with spies that have this logic inverted; an object uses `real` methods unless specified otherwise. We'll see and learn more about mocking soon when we start extending our Tic-Tac-Toe application. Right now, we'll take a look at one of the Java mocking frameworks called Mockito.

Mockito

Mockito is a mocking framework with a clean and simple API. Tests produced with Mockito are readable, easy-to-write, and intuitive. It contains three major static methods:

- `mock()`: This is used to create mocks. Optionally, we can specify how those mocks behave with `when()` and `given()`.
- `spy()`: This can be used for partial mocking. Spied objects invoke real methods unless we specify otherwise. As which `mock()`, behavior can be set for every public or protected method (excluding static). The major difference is that `mock()` creates a fake of the whole object, while `spy()` uses the *real* object.
- `verify()`: This is used to check whether methods were called with given arguments. It is a form of assert.

We'll go deeper into Mockito once we start coding our Tic-Tac-Toe v2 application. First, however , let us quickly go through a new set of requirements.

The Tic-Tac-Toe v2 requirements

The requirements of our *Tic-Tac-Toe v2* application are simple. We should add a persistent storage so that players can continue playing the game at some later time. We'll use MongoDB for this purpose.

[Add MongoDB persistent storage to the application.]

Developing Tic-Tac-Toe v2

We'll continue where we left off with Tic-Tac-Toe in *Chapter 3, Red-Green-Refactor: From Failure Through Success until Perfection*. The complete source code of the application developed so far can be found at https://bitbucket.org/vfarcic/ tdd-java-ch06-tic-tac-toe-mongo.git. Use the **VCS | Checkout from Version Control | Git** option from the **IntelliJ IDEA** to clone the code. As with any other project, the first thing we need to do is add the dependencies to build.gradle:

```
dependencies {
    compile 'org.jongo:jongo:1.1'
    compile 'org.mongodb:mongo-java-driver:2.+'
    testCompile 'junit:junit:4.11'
    testCompile 'org.mockito:mockito-all:1.+'
}
```

Importing the MongoDB driver should be self-explanatory. Jongo is a very helpful set of utility methods that make working with Java code in a way much more similar to the Mongo query language. For the testing part, we'll continue using JUnit with an addition of Mockito mocks, spies, and validations.

You'll notice that we won't install MongoDB until the very end. With Mockito, we will not need it, since all our Mongo dependencies will be mocked.

Once dependencies are specified, remember to refresh them in the IDEA **Gradle projects** dialogue.

The source code can be found in the 00-prerequisites branch of the tdd-java-ch06-tic-tac-toe-mongo Git repository (https://bitbucket.org/vfarcic/tdd-java-ch06-tic-tac-toe-mongo/branch/00-prerequisites).

Now that we have prerequisites set, let's start working on the first requirement.

Requirement 1

We should be able to save each move to the DB. Since we already have all the game logic implemented, this should be trivial to do. Nonetheless, this will be a very good example of mock usage.

 Implement an option to save a single move with the turn number, the X and Y axis positions, and the player (X or O).

Specification and specification implementation

We should start by defining the Java bean that will represent our data storage schema. There's nothing special about it, so we'll skip this part with only one note.

Do not spend too much time defining specifications for Java boilerplate code. Our implementation of the bean contains overwritten `equals` and `hashCode`. Both are generated automatically by IDEA and do not provide a real value, except to satisfy the need to compare two objects of the same type (we'll use that comparison later on in specifications). TDD is supposed to help us design better and write better code. Writing 15-20 specifications in order to define boilerplate code that could be written automatically by IDE (as is the case with the equals method), does not help us meet these objectives. Mastering TDD means not only learning how to write specifications, but also when it's not worth it.

That being said, consult the source code to see the bean specification and implementation in it's entirety.

The source code can be found in the `01-bean` branch of the `tdd-java-ch06-tic-tac-toe-mongo` Git repository (`https://bitbucket.org/vfarcic/tdd-java-ch06-tic-tac-toe-mongo/branch/01-bean`). Classes in particular are `TicTacToeBeanSpec` and `TicTacToeBean`.

Now let's go to a more interesting part (but still without mocks, spies, and validations). Let's write specifications related to saving data to MongoDB.

For this requirement, we'll create two new classes inside the `com.packtpublishing.tddjava.ch03tictactoe.mongo` package: `TicTacToeCollectionSpec` (inside `src/test/java`) and `TicTacToeCollection` (inside `src/main/java`).

Specification

We should specify what the name of the DB that we'll use will be:

```
@Test
public void
whenInstantiatedThenMongoHasDbNameTicTacToe() {
    TicTacToeCollection collection =
            new TicTacToeCollection();
    assertEquals(
            "tic-tac-toe",
            collection.getMongoCollection()
             .getDBCollection().getDB().getName());
}
```

We are instantiating a new `TicTacToeCollection` class and verifying that the DB name is what we expect.

Specification implementation

The implementation is very straightforward, as follows:

```
private MongoCollection mongoCollection;
protected MongoCollection getMongoCollection() {
    return mongoCollection;
}
public TicTacToeCollection()
        throws UnknownHostException {
    DB db = new MongoClient().getDB("tic-tac-toe");
    mongoCollection =
            new Jongo(db).getCollection("bla");
}
```

When instantiating the `TicTacToeCollection` class, we're creating a new `MongoCollection` with the specified DB name (`tic-tac-toe`) and assigning it to the local variable.

Bear with us. There's only one more specification left until we get to the interesting part where we'll use mocks and spies.

Specification

In the previous implementation, we used `bla` as the name of the collection because Jongo forced us to put some string. Let's create a specification that will define the name of the Mongo collection that we'll use:

```
@Test
public void
whenInstantiatedThenMongoCollectionHasNameGame() {
    TicTacToeCollection collection = new
            TicTacToeCollection();
    assertEquals(
            "game",
            collection.getMongoCollection()
                    .getName());
}
```

This specification is almost identical to the previous one and probably self-explanatory.

Implementation

All we have to do to implement this specification is change the string we used to set the collection name:

```
public TicTacToeCollection()
        throws UnknownHostException {
    DB db = new MongoClient().getDB("tic-tac-toe");
    mongoCollection =
            new Jongo(db).getCollection("game");
}
```

Refactoring

You might have got the impression that refactoring is reserved only for the implementation code. However, when we look the objectives behind refactoring (more readable, optimal, and faster code), they apply as much to specifications as to the implementation code.

The last two specifications have the instantiation of the TicTacToeCollection class repeated. We can move it to a method annotated with @Before. The effect will be the same (the class will be instantiated before each method annotated with @Test is run) and we'll remove the duplicated code. Since the same instantiation will be needed in further specs, removing duplication will now provide even more benefits later on. At the same time, we'll save ourselves from throwing UnknownHostException over and over again:

```
TicTacToeCollection collection;

@Before
public void before() throws UnknownHostException {
    collection = new TicTacToeCollection();
}
@Test
public void
whenInstantiatedThenMongoHasDbNameTicTacToe() {
//        throws UnknownHostException {
//    TicTacToeCollection collection = new
//    TicTacToeCollection();
        assertEquals("tic-tac-toe",
            collection.getMongoCollection()
                .getDBCollection().getDB()
                    .getName());
}
```

```
@Test
public void whenInstantiatedThenMongoHasNameGame()
{
//         throws UnknownHostException {
//     TicTacToeCollection collection = new
//     TicTacToeCollection();
    assertEquals("game",
            collection.getMongoCollection()
                .getName());
}
```

Use setup and teardown methods

Benefits: these allow preparation or setup and disposal or teardown code to be executed before and after the class or each test method.

In many cases, some code needs to be executed before the `test` class or each method in a class. For this purpose, JUnit has the `@BeforeClass` and `@Before` annotations that should be used in the setup phase. The `@BeforeClass` executes the associated method before the class is loaded (before the first test method is run). `@Before` executes the associated method before each test is run. Both should be used when there are certain preconditions required by tests. The most common example is setting up test data in the (hopefully in-memory) database. On the opposite end, are the `@After` and `@AfterClass` annotations that should be used as the teardown phase. Their main purpose is to destroy the data or state created during the setup phase or by tests themselves. Each test should be independent from others. Moreover, no test should be affected by the others. The teardown phase helps maintaining the system as if no test was previously executed.

Now let's do some mocking, spying, and verifying!

Specification

We should create a method that saves data to MongoDB. After studying Jongo documentation, we discovered that there is the `MongoCollection.save` method that does exactly that. It accepts any object as a method argument and transforms it (using Jackson) into JSON, which is natively used in MongoDB. The point is that after playing around with Jongo, we decided to use and, more importantly, trust this library.

We can write Mongo specifications in two ways. One more traditional and appropriate for **End2End (E2E)** or integration tests would be to bring up a MongoDB instance, invoke the Jongo's save method, query the database, and confirm that data has indeed been saved. It does not end here, as we would need to clean up the database before each test in order to always guarantee that the same state is unpolluted by the execution of previous tests. Finally, once all tests are finished executing, we might want to stop the MongoDB instance and free server resources for some other tasks.

As you might have guessed, there is quite a lot of work involved for a single test written in this way. Also, it's not only about work that needs to be invested into writing such tests. The execution time would be increased quite a lot. Running one test that communicates with a DB does not take long. Running ten tests is usually still fast. Running hundreds or thousands can take quite a lot of time. What happens when it takes a lot of time to run all unit tests? People lose patience and start dividing them into groups or give up on TDD all together. Dividing tests into groups means that we lose confidence that nothing got broken, since we are continuously testing only parts of it. Giving up on TDD... Well, that's not the objective we're trying to accomplish. However, if it takes a lot of time to run tests, it's reasonable to expect developers to not want to wait until they are finished running before they move to the next specification, and that is the point when we stop doing TDD. What is a reasonable amount of time to allow our unit tests to run? There is no one-fits-all rule that defines this; however, as a rule of thumb, if the time is longer than 10-15 seconds, we should start worrying, and dedicate time to optimizing them.

Tests should run fast

Benefits: tests are used often

If it takes a lot of time to run tests, developers will stop using them or run only a small subset related to the changes they are making. One benefit of fast tests, besides fostering their usage, is fast feedback. The sooner the problem is detected, the easier it is to fix it. Knowledge about the code that produced the problem is still fresh. If a developer has already started working on the next feature while waiting for the completion of the execution of tests, he might decide to postpone fixing the problem until that new feature is developed. On the other hand, if he drops his current work to fix the bug, time is lost in context switching.

If using live DB to run unit tests is not a good option, then what is the alternative? Mocking and spying! In our example, we know which method of a third-party library should be invoked. We also invested enough time to trust this library (besides integration tests that will be performed later on). Once we know how to use the library, we can limit our job to verifying that correct invocations of that library have been made.

Let us give it a try.

First, we should modify our existing code and convert our instantiation of the `TicTacToeCollection` into a spy:

```
import static org.mockito.Mockito.*;
...
@Before
public void before() throws UnknownHostException {
    collection = spy(new TicTacToeCollection());
}
```

Spying on a class is called **partial** mocking. When applied, the class will behave exactly the same as it would it was instantiated normally. The major difference is that we can apply partial mocking and substitute one or more methods with mocks. As a general rule, we tend to use spies mostly on classes that we're working on. We want to retain all the functionality of a class that we're writing specifications for, but with an additional option to, when needed, mock a part of it.

Now, let us write the specification itself. It could be the following:

```
@Test
public void
whenSaveMoveThenInvokeMongoCollectionSave() {
    TicTacToeBean bean =
            new TicTacToeBean(3, 2, 1, 'Y');
    MongoCollection mongoCollection =
            mock(MongoCollection.class);
    doReturn(mongoCollection).when(collection)
            .getMongoCollection();
    collection.saveMove(bean);
    verify(mongoCollection, times(1)).save(bean);
}
```

Static methods such as `mock`, `doReturn`, and `verify` are all from the `org.mockito.Mockito` class.

First, we're creating a new `TicTacToeBean`. There's nothing special there. Next, we are creating a mock object out of the `MongoCollection`. Since we already established that, when working on a unit level, we want to avoid direct communication with the DB, mocking this dependency will provide this for us. It will convert a `real` class into a mocked one. For the class using `mongoCollection`, it'll look like a *real* one; however, behind the scenes, all its methods are *shallow* and do not actually do anything. It's like overwriting that class and replacing all the methods with empty ones:

```
MongoCollection mongoCollection =
        mock(MongoCollection.class);
```

Next, we're telling that mocked `mongoCollection` should be returned whenever we call the `getMongoCollection` method of the collection spied class. In other words, we're telling our class to use a fake collection instead of the real one:

```
    doReturn(mongoCollection).when(collection)
    .getMongoCollection();
```

Then, we're calling the method that we are working on:

```
    collection.saveMove(bean);
```

Finally, we should verify that the correct invocation of the `Jongo` library is performed once:

```
    verify(mongoCollection, times(1)).save(bean);
```

Let's try to implement this specification.

Specification implementation

In order to better understand the specification we just wrote, let us do only partial implementation. We'll create an empty method, `saveMove`. This will allow our code to compile without implementing the specification yet:

```
public void saveMove(TicTacToeBean bean) {
}
```

When we run our specifications (`gradle` test), the result is the following:

```
Wanted but not invoked:
mongoCollection.save(
    Turn: 3; X: 2; Y: 1; Player: Y
);
```

Mockito tells us that, according to our specification, we expect the
mongoCollection.save method to be invoked, and that the expectation was
not fulfilled. Since the test is still failing, we need to go back and finish the
implementation. One of the biggest sins in TDD is to have a failing test and move
onto something else.

All tests should pass before a new test is written

Benefits: focus is maintained on a small unit of work, and implementation
code is (almost) always in a working condition.

It is sometimes tempting to write multiple tests before the actual
implementation. In other cases, developers ignore problems detected by
the existing tests and move towards new features. This should be avoided
whenever possible. In most cases, breaking this rule will only introduce
technical debt that will need to be paid with interest. One of the goals of
TDD is ensuring that the implementation code is (almost) always working
as expected. Some projects, due to pressures to reach the delivery date or
maintain the budget, break this rule and dedicate time to new features,
leaving the fixing of the code associated with failed tests for later. Those
projects usually end up postponing the inevitable.

Let's modify the implementation to, for example, the following:

```
public void saveMove(TicTacToeBean bean) {
    getMongoCollection().save(null);
}
```

If we run our specifications again, the result is the following:

```
Argument(s) are different! Wanted:
mongoCollection.save(
    Turn: 3; X: 2; Y: 1; Player: Y
);
```

This time we are invoking the expected method, but the arguments we are passing
to it are not what we hoped for. In the specification, we set the expectation to a
bean (new TicTacToeBean(3, 2, 1, 'Y')) and in the implementation, we passed
null. Not only that Mockito verifications can tell us whether a correct method was
invoked, but also whether arguments passed to that method are correct.

The correct implementation of the specification is the following:

```
public void saveMove(TicTacToeBean bean) {
    getMongoCollection().save(bean);
}
```

This time all specifications should pass, and we can, happily, proceed to the next one.

Specification

Let us change the return type of our `saveMove` method to `boolean`:

```
@Test
public void whenSaveMoveThenReturnTrue() {
    TicTacToeBean bean =
            new TicTacToeBean(3, 2, 1, 'Y');
    MongoCollection mongoCollection =
            mock(MongoCollection.class);
    doReturn(mongoCollection).when(collection)
            .getMongoCollection();
    assertTrue(collection.saveMove(bean));
}
```

Specification implementation

This implementation is very straightforward. We should change the method return type. Remember that one of the rules of TDD is to use the simplest possible solution. The simplest solution is to return `true` as in the following example:

```
public boolean saveMove(TicTacToeBean bean) {
    getMongoCollection().save(bean);
    return true;
}
```

Refactoring

You have probably noticed that the last two specifications have the first two lines duplicated. We can refactor the specifications code by moving them to the method annotated with `@Before`:

```
TicTacToeCollection collection;
TicTacToeBean bean;
MongoCollection mongoCollection;

@Before
public void before() throws UnknownHostException {
    collection = spy(new TicTacToeCollection());
    bean = new TicTacToeBean(3, 2, 1, 'Y');
    mongoCollection = mock(MongoCollection.class);
}
...
@Test
public void
```

```
whenSaveMoveThenInvokeMongoCollectionSave() {
//    TicTacToeBean bean =
//    new TicTacToeBean(3, 2, 1, 'Y');
//    MongoCollection mongoCollection =
//        mock(MongoCollection.class);
    doReturn(mongoCollection).when(collection)
            .getMongoCollection();
    collection.saveMove(bean);
    verify(mongoCollection, times(1)).save(bean);
}

@Test
public void whenSaveMoveThenReturnTrue() {
//    TicTacToeBean bean =
//    new TicTacToeBean(3, 2, 1, 'Y');
//    MongoCollection mongoCollection =
//        mock(MongoCollection.class);
    doReturn(mongoCollection).when(collection)
            .getMongoCollection();
    assertTrue(collection.saveMove(bean));
}
```

Specification

Now let us contemplate the option that something might go wrong when using MongoDB. When, for example, an exception is thrown, we might want to return `false` from our `saveMove` method:

```
@Test
public void
givenExceptionWhenSaveMoveThenReturnFalse() {
    doThrow(new MongoException("Bla"))
            .when(mongoCollection)
            .save(any(TicTacToeBean.class));
    doReturn(mongoCollection).when(collection)
        .getMongoCollection();
    assertFalse(collection.saveMove(bean));
}
```

Here we introduce to another `Mockito` method: `doThrow`. It acts in a similar way to `doReturn` and throws an `Exception` when conditions set in when are fulfilled. The specification will throw the `MongoException` when the save method inside the `mongoCollection` class is invoked. This allows us to assert that our `saveMove` method returns `false` when an exception is thrown.

Specification implementation

The implementation can be as simple as adding a `try`/`catch` block:

```
public boolean saveMove(TicTacToeBean bean) {
    try {
        getMongoCollection().save(bean);
        return true;
    } catch (Exception e) {
        return false;
    }
}
```

Specification

This is a very simple application that, at least at this moment, can store only one game session. Whenever a new instance is created, we should start over and remove all data stored in the database. The easiest way to do this is to simply drop the MongoDB collection. Jongo has the `MongoCollection.drop()` method that can be used for that. We'll create a new method drop that will act in a similar way to `saveMove`.

If you haven't worked with Mockito, MongoDB, and/or Jongo, chances are you were not able to do the exercises from this chapter by yourself and just decided to follow the solutions we provided. If that's the case, this is the moment when you might want to switch gears and try to write specifications and the implementation by yourself.

We should verify that `MongoCollection.drop()` is invoked from our own method `drop()` inside the `TicTacToeCollection` class. Try it by yourself before looking at the following code. It should be almost the same as what we did with the `save` method:

```
@Test
public void
whenDropThenInvokeMongoCollectionDrop() {
    doReturn(mongoCollection).when(collection)
            .getMongoCollection();
    collection.drop();
    verify(mongoCollection).drop();
}
```

Specification implementation

Since this is a wrapper method, implementing this specification should be fairly easy:

```
public void drop() {
    getMongoCollection().drop();
}
```

Specification

We're almost done with this class. There are only two specifications left.

Let us make sure that in normal circumstances we return `true`:

```
@Test
public void whenDropThenReturnTrue() {
    doReturn(mongoCollection).when(collection)
            .getMongoCollection();
    assertTrue(collection.drop());
}
```

Specification implementation

If things look too easy with TDD, then that is on purpose. We are splitting tasks into such small entities that, in most cases, implementing a specification is a piece of cake. This one is no exception:

```
public boolean drop() {
    getMongoCollection().drop();
    return true;
}
```

Specification

Finally, let us make sure that the `drop` method returns `false` in case of an `Exception`:

```
@Test
public void
givenExceptionWhenDropThenReturnFalse() {
    doThrow(new MongoException("Bla"))
            .when(mongoCollection)
            .drop();
    doReturn(mongoCollection).when(collection)
            .getMongoCollection();
    assertFalse(collection.drop());
}
```

Specification implementation

Let us just add a try/catch block:

```
public boolean drop() {
    try {
        getMongoCollection().drop();
        return true;
    } catch (Exception e) {
        return false;
    }
}
```

With this implementation, we are finished with the TicTacToeCollection class that acts as a layer between our main class and MongoDB.

The source code can be found in the 02-save-move branch of the tdd-java-ch06-tic-tac-toe-mongo Git repository (https://bitbucket.org/vfarcic/tdd-java-ch06-tic-tac-toe-mongo/branch/02-save-move). The classes in particular are TicTacToeCollectionSpec and TicTacToeCollection.

Requirement 2

Let us employ the TicTacToeCollection methods inside our main class TicTacToe. Whenever a player plays a turn successfully, we should save it to the DB. Also, we should drop the collection whenever a new class is instantiated so that a new game does not overlap the old one. We could make it much more elaborate than this; however, for the purpose of this chapter and learning how to use mocking, this requirement should do for now.

 Save each turn to the database and make sure that a new session cleans the old data.

Let's do some set up first.

Specification

Since all our methods that should be used to communicate with MongoDB are in the TicTacToeCollection class, we should make sure that it is instantiated. The specification could be the following:

```
@Test
public void whenInstantiatedThenSetCollection() {
    assertNotNull(
            ticTacToe.getTicTacToeCollection());
}
```

The instantiation of `TicTacToe` is already done in the method annotated with `@Before`. With this specification, we're making sure that the collection is instantiated as well.

Specification implementation

There is nothing special about this implementation. We should simply overwrite the default constructor and assign a new instance to the `ticTacToeCollection` variable.

To begin with, we should add a local variable and a getter for `TicTacToeCollection`:

```
private TicTacToeCollection ticTacToeCollection;

protected TicTacToeCollection
        getTicTacToeCollection() {
    return ticTacToeCollection;
}
```

Now, all that's left is to instantiate a new collection and assign it to the variable when the main class is instantiated:

```
public TicTacToe() throws UnknownHostException {
    this(new TicTacToeCollection());
}
protected TicTacToe
        (TicTacToeCollection collection) {
    ticTacToeCollection = collection;
}
```

We also created another way to instantiate the class by passing `TicTacToeCollection` as an argument. This will come in handy inside specifications as an easy way to pass mocked collection.

Now let us go back to the specifications class and make use of this new constructor.

Specification refactoring

To utilize a newly created `TicTacToe` constructor, we can do something like the following:

```
private TicTacToeCollection collection;

@Before
public final void before()
        throws UnknownHostException {
```

```
        collection = mock(TicTacToeCollection.class);
//      ticTacToe = new TicTacToe();
        ticTacToe = new TicTacToe(collection);
}
```

Now all our specifications will use a mocked version of the `TicTacToeCollection`. There are other ways to inject mocked dependencies (for example, with Spring); however, when possible, we feel that simplicity trumps complicated frameworks.

Specification

Whenever we play a turn, it should be saved to the DB. The specification can be the following:

```
@Test
public void whenPlayThenSaveMoveIsInvoked() {
    TicTacToeBean move =
            new TicTacToeBean(1, 1, 3, 'X');
    ticTacToe.play(move.getX(), move.getY());
    verify(collection).saveMove(move);
}
```

By now, you should be familiar with Mockito, but let us go through the code as a refresher:

1. First, we are instantiating a `TicTacToeBean` since it contains data that our collections expect:

    ```
    TicTacToeBean move = new TicTacToeBean(1, 1, 3, 'X');
    ```

2. Next, it is time to play an actual turn:

    ```
    ticTacToe.play(move.getX(), move.getY());
    ```

3. Finally, we need to verify that the `saveMove` method is really invoked:

    ```
    verify(collection, times(1)).saveMove(move);
    ```

As we did throughout this chapter, we isolated all external invocations and focused only on the unit (`play`) that we're working on. Keep in mind that this isolation is limited only to the `public` and `protected` methods. When it comes to the actual implementation, we might choose to add the `saveMove` invocation to the `play` `public` method or one of the `private` methods that we wrote as a result of the refactoring we did earlier.

Specification implementation

This specification poses a couple of challenges. First, where should we place the invocation of the saveMove method? The setBox private method looks like a good place. That's where we are doing validations of whether the turn is valid, and if it is, we can call the saveMove method. However, that method expects a bean instead of variables x, y, and lastPlayer that are being used right now, so we might want to change the signature of the setBox method.

This is how the method looks now:

```
private void setBox(int x, int y, char lastPlayer)
{
    if (board[x - 1][y - 1] != '\0') {
        throw new RuntimeException(
                "Box is occupied");
    } else {
        board[x - 1][y - 1] = lastPlayer;
    }
}
```

This is how it looks after the necessary changes are applied:

```
private void setBox(TicTacToeBean bean) {
    if (board[bean.getX() - 1][bean.getY() - 1]
            != '\0') {
        throw new RuntimeException(
                "Box is occupied");
    } else {
        board[bean.getX() - 1][bean.getY() - 1] =
                lastPlayer;
        getTicTacToeCollection().saveMove(bean);
    }
}
```

The change of the setBox signature triggers a few other changes. Since it is invoked from the play method, we'll need to instantiate the bean there:

```
public String play(int x, int y) {
    checkAxis(x);
    checkAxis(y);
    lastPlayer = nextPlayer();
//    setBox(x, y, lastPlayer);
    setBox(new TicTacToeBean(1, x, y, lastPlayer));
    if (isWin(x, y)) {
        return lastPlayer + " is the winner";
```

```
        } else if (isDraw()) {
            return RESULT_DRAW;
        } else {
            return NO_WINNER;
        }
    }
}
```

You might have noticed that we used a constant value 1 as a turn. There is still no specification that says otherwise, so we took a shortcut. We'll deal with it later.

All those changes were still very simple, and it took a reasonably short period of time to implement them. If the changes were bigger, we might have chosen a different path; make a simpler change and get to the final solution through refactoring. Remember that the speed is the key. You don't want to get stuck with the implementation that does not pass tests for a long time.

Specification

What happens if a move could not be saved? Our helper method saveMove returns true or false depending on the MongoDB operation outcome. We might want to throw an exception when it returns false.

First things first; we should change the implementation of the before method and make sure that, by default, saveMove returns true:

```
@Before
public final void before()
        throws UnknownHostException {
    collection = mock(TicTacToeCollection.class);
    doReturn(true)
            .when(collection)
            .saveMove(any(TicTacToeBean.class));
    ticTacToe = new TicTacToe(collection);
}
```

Now that we stubbed the mocked collection with what we think is the default behavior (return true when saveMove is invoked), we can proceed and write the specification:

```
@Test
public void
whenPlayAndSaveReturnsFalseThenThrowException() {
    doReturn(false).when(collection).
            saveMove(any(TicTacToeBean.class));
    TicTacToeBean move =
            new TicTacToeBean(1, 1, 3, 'X');
```

```
        exception.expect(RuntimeException.class);
        ticTacToe.play(move.getX(), move.getY());
    }
```

We're using Mockito to return `false` when `saveMove` is invoked. Since, in this case, we don't care about a specific invocation of `saveMove`, we used `any(TicTacToeBean.class)` as the method argument. This is another one of Mockito's static methods.

Once everything is set, we use a JUnit expectation in the same way as we did before throughout the *Chapter 3, Red-Green-Refactor - From Failure Through Success until Perfection* .

Specification implementation

Let's do a simple if and throw a `RuntimeException` when the result is not expected:

```
    private void setBox(TicTacToeBean bean) {
        if (board[bean.getX() - 1][bean.getY() - 1]
                != '\0') {
            throw new RuntimeException(
                    "Box is occupied");
        } else {
            board[bean.getX() - 1][bean.getY() - 1] =
                    lastPlayer;
//          getTicTacToeCollection().saveMove(bean);
            if (!getTicTacToeCollection()
                    .saveMove(bean)) {
                throw new RuntimeException(
                        "Saving to DB failed");
            }
        }
    }
```

Specification

Do you remember the turn that we hard coded to be always 1? Let's fix that behavior.

We can invoke the `play` method twice and verify that the turn changes from 1 to 2:

```
    @Test
    public void
    whenPlayInvokedMultipleTimesThenTurnIncreases() {
        TicTacToeBean move1 =
                new TicTacToeBean(1, 1, 1, 'X');
```

```
ticTacToe.play(move1.getX(), move1.getY());
verify(collection, times(1)).saveMove(move1);
TicTacToeBean move2 =
        new TicTacToeBean(2, 1, 2, 'O');
ticTacToe.play(move2.getX(), move2.getY());
verify(collection, times(1)).saveMove(move2);
}
```

Specification implementation

As with almost everything else done in the TDD fashion, implementation is fairly easy:

```
private int turn = 0;
...
public String play(int x, int y) {
    checkAxis(x);
    checkAxis(y);
    lastPlayer = nextPlayer();
    setBox(new TicTacToeBean(++turn, x, y,
            lastPlayer));
    if (isWin(x, y)) {
        return lastPlayer + " is the winner";
    } else if (isDraw()) {
        return RESULT_DRAW;
    } else {
        return NO_WINNER;
    }
}
```

Exercises

A few more specifications and their implementations are still missing. We should invoke the drop() method whenever our TicTacToe class is instantiated. We should also make sure that RuntimeException is thrown when drop() returns false. We'll leave those specifications and their implementations as an exercise for you.

The source code can be found in the 03-mongo branch of the tdd-java-ch06-tic-tac-toe-mongo Git repository (https://bitbucket.org/vfarcic/tdd-java-ch06-tic-tac-toe-mongo/branch/03-mongo). The classes in particular are TicTacToeSpec and TicTacToe.

Integration tests

We did a lot of unit tests. We relied a lot on trust. Unit after unit was specified and implemented. While working on specifications, we isolated everything but the units we were working on, and verified that one invoked the other correctly. However, the time has come to validate that all those units are truly able to communicate with MongoDB. We might have made a mistake or, more importantly, we might not have MongoDB up and running. It would be a disaster to discover that, for example, we deployed our application, but forgot to bring up the DB, or that the configuration (IP, port, and so on) is not set correctly.

The integration tests' objective is to validate, as you might have guessed, the integration of separate components, applications, systems, and so on. If you remember the testing pyramid, it states that unit tests are the easiest to write and fastest to run, so we should keep other types of tests limited to things that UTs did not cover.

We should isolate our integration tests in a way that they can be run occasionally (before we push our code to repository, or as a part of our Continuous Integration process) and keep unit test as a continuous feedback loop.

Tests separation

If we follow some kind of convention, it is fairly easy to separate tests in Gradle. We can have our tests in different directories and distinct packages or, for example, with different file suffixes. In this case, we choose the later. All our specification classes are named with the `Spec` suffix (that is, `TicTacToeSpec`). We can make a rule that all integration tests have the `Integ` suffix.

With that in mind, let us modify our `build.gradle` file.

First, we'll tell Gradle that only classes ending with `Spec` should be used by the `test` task:

```
test {

    include '**/*Spec.class'
}
```

Next, we can create a new task `testInteg`:

```
task testInteg(type: Test) {
    include '**/*Integ.class'
}
```

With those two additions to the `build.gradle`, we continue having the test tasks that we used heavily throughout the book; however, this time, limited only to specifications (unit tests). In addition, all integration tests can be run by clicking the `testInteg` task from the Gradle projects IDEA window or running the following command from command prompt:

```
gradle testInteg
```

Let us write a simple integration test.

The integration test

We'll create a `TicTacToeInteg` class inside the `com.packtpublishing.tddjava.ch03tictactoe` package in the `src/test/java` directory. Since we know that Jongo throws an exception if it cannot connect to the database, a test class can be as simple as the following:

```
import org.junit.Test;
import java.net.UnknownHostException;
import static org.junit.Assert.*;

public class TicTacToeInteg {

    @Test
    public void
        givenMongoDbIsRunningWhenPlayThenNoException()
            throws UnknownHostException {
        TicTacToe ticTacToe = new TicTacToe();
        assertEquals(TicTacToe.NO_WINNER,
        ticTacToe.play(1, 1));
    }

}
```

The invocation of assertEquals is just as a precaution. The real objective of this test is to make sure that no Exception is thrown. Since we did not start MongoDB (unless you are very proactive and did it yourself, in which case you should stop it), test should fail.

```
×  −  □    vfarcic@viktor: ~/IdeaProjects/tdd-java-ch06-tic-tac-toe-mongo

vfarcic@viktor:~/IdeaProjects/tdd-java-ch06-tic-tac-toe-mongo$ gradle testInteg
:compileJava UP-TO-DATE
:processResources UP-TO-DATE
:classes UP-TO-DATE
:compileTestJava UP-TO-DATE
:processTestResources UP-TO-DATE
:testClasses UP-TO-DATE
:testInteg

com.packtpublishing.tddjava.ch03tictactoe.TicTacToeInteg > givenMongoDbIsRunning
WhenPlayThenNoException                                                         F
AILED
    java.lang.RuntimeException at TicTacToeInteg.java:12

1 test completed, 1 failed
:testInteg FAILED

FAILURE: Build failed with an exception.

* What went wrong:
Execution failed for task ':testInteg'.
> There were failing tests. See the report at: file:///home/vfarcic/IdeaProjects
/tdd-java-ch06-tic-tac-toe-mongo/build/reports/tests/index.html

* Try:
Run with --stacktrace option to get the stack trace. Run with --info or --debug
option to get more log output.

BUILD FAILED

Total time: 14.6 secs
vfarcic@viktor:~/IdeaProjects/tdd-java-ch06-tic-tac-toe-mongo$ █
```

Now that we know that the integration test works, or in other words, that it indeed fails when MongoDB is not up and running, let us try it again with the DB started. To bring up MongoDB, we'll use Vagrant to create a virtual machine with Ubuntu OS. MongoDB will be run as a docker.

Make sure that the 04-integration branch is checked out:

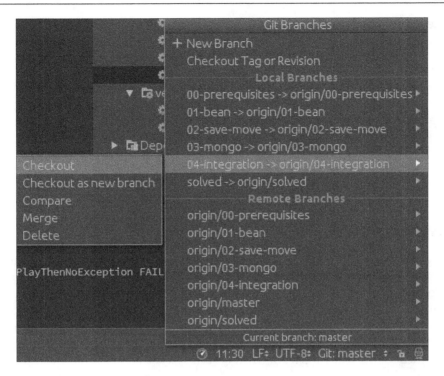

From the command prompt, run the following command:

```
$ vagrant up
```

Be patient until VM is up and running (it might take a while when executed for the first time, especially on a slower bandwidth). Once finished, rerun integration tests.

```
×  −  □   vfarcic@viktor: ~/IdeaProjects/tdd-java-ch06-tic-tac-toe-mongo
vfarcic@viktor:~/IdeaProjects/tdd-java-ch06-tic-tac-toe-mongo$ gradle testInteg
:compileJava UP-TO-DATE
:processResources UP-TO-DATE
:classes UP-TO-DATE
:compileTestJava UP-TO-DATE
:processTestResources UP-TO-DATE
:testClasses UP-TO-DATE
:testInteg

BUILD SUCCESSFUL

Total time: 4.46 secs
vfarcic@viktor:~/IdeaProjects/tdd-java-ch06-tic-tac-toe-mongo$ ▯
```

It worked, and now we're confident that we are indeed integrated with MongoDB.

This was a very simplistic integration test, and in the *real world*, we would do a bit more than this single test. We could, for example, query the DB and confirm that data was stored correctly. However, the purpose of this chapter was to learn both how to mock and that we should not depend only on unit tests. The next chapter will explore integration and functional tests in more depth.

The source code can be found in the `04-integration` branch of the `tdd-java-ch06-tic-tac-toe-mongo` Git repository (`https://bitbucket.org/vfarcic/tdd-java-ch06-tic-tac-toe-mongo/branch/04-integration`).

Summary

Mocking and spying techniques are used to isolate different parts of code or third-party libraries. They are essential if we are to proceed with great speed, not only while coding, but also while running tests. Tests without mocks are often too complex to write and can be so slow that, with time, TDD tends to become close to impossible. Slow tests mean that we won't be able to run all of them every time we write a new specification. That in itself leads to deterioration in confidence we have in the our tests, since only a part of them is run.

Mocking is not only useful as a way to isolate external dependencies, but also as a way to isolate our own code from a unit we're working on.

In this chapter, we presented Mockito as, in our opinion, the framework with the best balance between functionality and ease of use. We invite you to investigate its documentation in more detail (`http://mockito.org/`), as well as other Java frameworks dedicated to mocking. EasyMock (`http://easymock.org/`), JMock (`http://www.jmock.org/`), and PowerMock (`https://code.google.com/p/powermock/`) are few of the most popular.

7
BDD – Working Together with the Whole Team

"I'm not a great programmer; I'm just a good programmer with great habits."

- Kent Beck

Everything we did until now is related to techniques that can be applied only by developers for developers. Customers, business representatives, and other parties that are not capable of reading and understanding code were not involved in the process.

TDD can be much more than what we did until now. We can define requirements, discuss them with the client, and get agreement as to what should be developed. We can use those same requirements and make them executable so that they drive and validate our development. We can use ubiquitous language to write acceptance criteria. All this, and more, is accomplished with a flavor of TDD called behavior-driven development (BDD).

We'll develop a **Books Store** application using a BDD approach. We'll define acceptance criteria in English, make the implementation of each feature separately, confirm that it is working correctly by running BDD scenarios and, if required, refactor the code to accomplish the desired level of quality. The process still follows the red-green-refactor that is the essence of TDD. The major difference is the definition level. While until this moment, we were mostly working at units level, this time we'll move a bit higher and apply TDD through functional and integration tests.

Our frameworks of choice will be JBehave and Selenide.

The following topics will be covered in this chapter:

- The different specifications
- Behavior-driven development (BDD)
- The Books Store BDD story
- JBehave

Different specifications

We already mentioned that one of the benefits of TDD is executable documentation that is always up to date. However, documentation obtained through unit tests is often not enough. When working at such a low level, we get insights into details; however, it is all too easy to miss the big picture. If, for example, you were to inspect specifications that we created for the Tic-Tac-Toe game, you might easily miss the point of the application. You would understand what each unit does and how it interoperates with other units, but would have a hard time grasping the idea behind it. To be precise, you would understand that unit X does Y and communicates with Z; however, the functional documentation and the idea behind it would be, at best, hard to find.

The same can be said for development. Before we start working on specifications in the form of unit tests, we need to get a bigger picture. Throughout this book, you were presented with requirements that we used for writing specifications that resulted in their implementation. Those requirements were later on discarded; they are nowhere to be seen. We did not put them to the repository, nor did we use them to validate the result of our work.

Documentation

In many organizations that we worked with, the documentation was created for the wrong reasons. The management tends to think that documentation is somehow related to project success; that without a lot of (often short-lived) documentation, the project will fail. Thus, we are asked to spend a lot of time planning, answering questions, and filling in questionnaires that are often designed not to help the project but to provide an illusion that everything is under control. Someone's existence is often justified with documentation (the result of my work is this document). It also serves as a reassurance that everything is going as planned (there is an Excel sheet that states that we are on schedule). However, by far the most common reason for the creation of documentation is a process that simply states that certain documents need to be created. We might question the value of those documents; however, since the process is sacred, they need to be produced.

Not only that documentation might be created for the wrong reasons and might not provide enough value, but, as is often the case, it might also do a lot of damage. If we created the documentation, it is natural that we trust it. However, what happens if that documentation is not up to date? The requirements are changing, bugs are getting fixed, new functionalities are being developed, and some are being removed. If given enough time, all traditional documentation becomes obsolete. The sheer task of updating documentation with every change we make to the code is so big and complex that, sooner or later, we must face the fact that static documents do not reflect the reality. If we are putting our trust into something that is not accurate, our development is based on wrong assumptions.

The only accurate documentation is our code. The code is what we develop, what we deploy, and is the only source that truthfully represents our application. However, code is not readable by everyone involved with the project. Besides coders, we might work with managers, testers, business people, end users, and so on.

In search of a better way to define what would constitute better documentation, let us explore a bit further who are the potential documentation consumers. For the sake of simplicity, we'll divide them into coders (those capable of reading and understanding code) and non-coders (everyone else).

Documentation for coders

Developers work with code and, since we established that code is the most accurate documentation, there is no reason to not utilize it. If you want to understand what some method does, take a look at the code of that method. Having doubt about what some class does? Take a look at that class. Having trouble understanding a piece of code? We have a problem! However, the problem is not that the documentation is missing, but that the code itself is not written well.

Looking at the code to understand the code is still often not enough. Even though you might understand what the code does, the purpose of that code might not be so obvious. Why was it written in the first place?

That's where specifications come in. Not only are we using them to continuously validate the code, but they also act as executable documentation. They are always up to date because if they aren't, their execution will fail. At the same time, while code itself should be written in a way that is easy to read and understand, specifications provide a much easier and faster way to understand the reasons, logic, and motivations that lead us to write some piece of implementation code.

Using code as documentation does not exclude other types. Quite the contrary, the key is not to avoid using static documentation, but to avoid duplication. When code provides the necessary details, use it before anything else. In most cases, this leaves us with higher-level documentation such as an overview, the general purpose of the system, the technologies used, the environment set-up, installation, building, packaging and other types of data that tend to serve more like guidelines and quick-start than detailed information. For those cases, a simple README in markdown format (`http://whatismarkdown.com/`) tends to the best.

For all code-based documentation, test-driven development is the `best.enabler`. Until now, we worked only with units (methods). We are yet to see how to apply TDD on a higher level such as, for example, functional specifications. However, before we get there, let's speak about other roles in the team.

Documentation for non-coders

Traditional testers tend to form groups completely separated from developers. This separation leads to increased number of testers who are not familiar with code and assume that their job is to be quality checkers. They are validators at the end of the process and act as a kind of border police that decides what can be deployed and what should be returned back. There is, on the other hand, an increasing number of organizations that are employing testers as integral members of the team with the job of ensuring that quality is built in. This latter group requires testers to be proficient with code. For them, using code as documentation is quite natural. However, what should we do with the first group? What should we do with testers who do not understand the code? Also, it is not only (some) testers that fall into this group. Managers, end-users, business representatives, and so on, are also included. The world is full of people that cannot read and understand code.

We should look for a way to retain the advantages that the executable documentation provides, but write it in a way that can be understood by everyone. Moreover, in the TDD fashion, we should allow everyone to participate in the creation of executable documentation from the very start. We should allow them to define requirements that we'll use to develop applications and, at the same time, to validate the result of that development. We need something that will define what we'll do on a higher level, since low level is already covered with unit tests. To summarize, we need a documentation that can serve as requirements, that can be executed, that can validate our work, and that can be written and understood by everyone.

Say hello to behavior-driven development (BDD).

Behavior-driven development

BDD is an agile process designed to keep the focus on stakeholder value throughout the whole project. It is a form of TDD. Specifications are defined in advance, the implementation is done according to those specifications, and they are run periodically to validate the outcome. Besides those similarities, there are a few differences as well. Unlike in TDD, which is based on unit tests, BDD encourages us to write multiple specifications (called scenarios) before starting the implementation (coding). Even though there is no specific rule, BDD tends to levitate towards higher-level functional requirements. While it can be employed at a unit level as well, the real benefits are obtained when taking a higher approach that can be written and understood by everyone. The audience is another difference: BDD tries to empower everyone (coders, testers, managers, end users, business representatives, and so on). While TDD, which is based on unit level, can be described as inside-out (we begin with units and build up towards functionalities), BDD is often understood as outside-in (we start with features and go inside towards units). Behavior-driven development acts as an acceptance criteria on that acts as an indicator of readiness. It tells us when something is finished and ready for production.

We start by defining functionalities (or behaviors), work on them by employing TDD with unit tests and, once a complete behavior has finished, validate with BDD. One BDD scenario can take hours or even days to finish. During all that time, we can employ TDD and unit testing. Once we're done, we run BDD scenarios to do the final validation. TDD is for coders and has a very fast cycle, while BDD is for everyone and has a much slower turnout time. For each BDD scenario, we have many TDD unit tests.

At this point, you might have gotten confused about what BDD really is, so let us go back a bit. We'll start with the explanation of its format.

Narrative

A BDD story consists of one narrative followed by at least one scenario. A narrative is only informative, and its main purpose is to provide just enough information that should serve as a beginning of a communication between everyone involved (testers, business representatives, developers, analysts, and so on). It is a short and simple description of a feature told from the perspective of a person that requires it.

The goal of a narrative is to answer three basic questions:

1. What is the benefit or value of the feature that should be built (*In order to*)?
2. Who needs the feature that was requested (*As a*)?
3. What is the feature or goal that should be developed (*I want to*)?

Once we have those questions answered, we can start defining what we think would be the best solution. That thinking process results in scenarios that provide a lower level of details.

Until now, we were working at a very low level using unit tests as a driving force. We were specifying what should be built from the coders' perspective. We assumed that high-level requirements were defined earlier and that our job was to do the code specific to one of them. Now, let us take a few steps back and start from the beginning. Let us act, let's say, as a customer or a business representative. Someone got this great idea and we are discussing it with the rest of the team. In short, we want to build an online book store. It is only an idea and we're not even certain of how it will develop, so we want to work on a **Minimum Viable Product (MVP)**. One of the roles that we want to explore is the one of a store administrator. This person should be able to add new books and update or remove the existing ones. All those actions should be doable, because we want this person to be able to manage our book store collection in an efficient way. The narrative that we came up with for this role is the following:

```
In order to manage the book store collection efficiently
As a store administrator
I want to be able to add, update and remove books
```

Now we know what is the benefit (*manage books*), who needs it (*administrator*), and finally what is the feature that should be developed (*insert*, *update*, and *delete* operations). Keep in mind that this was not a detailed description of what should be done. The narrative's purpose is to initiate a discussion that will result in one or more scenarios.

Unlike TDD unit tests, narrative, and indeed the rest of the BDD story, can be written by anyone. They do not require coding skills, nor do they have to go into too many details. Depending on the organization, all narratives can be written by the same person (a business representative, product owner, customer, and so on) or it might be a collaborative effort by the whole team.

Now that we have a bit clearer idea regarding narratives, let us take a look at scenarios.

Scenarios

A narrative acts as a communication enabler and scenarios are the result of that communication. They should describe interactions that the role (specified in the *As a* section) has with the system. Unlike unit tests, which were written as code by developers for developers, BDD scenarios should be defined in plain language and with minimum technical details so that all those involved with the project (developers, testers, designers, managers, customers, and so on) can have a common understanding about behaviors (or features) that will be added to the system.

Scenarios act as the acceptance criteria of the narrative. Once all scenarios related to the narrative are run successfully, the job can be considered done. Each scenario is very similar to a unit test, with the main difference being the scope (one method against a whole feature) and time it takes to implement it (a few seconds or minutes against a few hours or even days). Similarly to unit tests, scenarios drive the development. They are defined first.

Each scenario consists of a description and one or more steps that start with the words *Given*, *When*, or *Then*. The description is short and only informative. It helps us to understand at a glance what the scenario does. Steps, on the other hand, are a sequence of preconditions, events, and expected outcomes of the scenario. They help us define the behavior unambiguously and it's easy to translate them to automated tests.

Throughout this chapter, we'll focus more on the technical aspects of BDD and the ways they fit into the developers' mindset. For broader usage of BDD and much deeper discussion, consult the book specification by Example: *How Successful Teams Deliver the Right Software* by *Gojko Adzic*.

The *Given* step defines a context or preconditions that need to be fulfilled for the rest of the scenario to be successful. Going back to the book's administration narrative, one such precondition might be the following:

```
Given user is on the books screen
```

This is a very simple but pretty necessary precondition. Our website might have many pages and we need to make sure that the user is on the correct screen before we perform any action.

The *When* step defines an action or some kind of an event. In our narrative, we defined that the administrator should be able to add, update, and remove books. Let's see what should be an action related to, for example, the delete operation:

```
When user selects a book
When user clicks the deleteBook button
```

In this example, we multiplied actions defined with the *When* steps. First, we should select a book and then we should click on the **Delete the book** button. In this case, we used an ID (`deleteBook`) instead of text (Delete the book) to define the button that should be clicked. In most cases, IDs are preferable because they provide multiple benefits. They are unique (only one ID can exist on a given screen), they provide clear instruction for developers (create an element with an ID `deleteBook`), and they are not affected by other changes on the same screen. The text of an element can easily change; if this happens, all scenarios that used it would fail as well. In the case of websites, an alternative could be XPath. However, avoid it whenever possible. It tends to fail with the smallest change to the HTML structure.

Similarly to unit tests, scenarios should be reliable and fail when a feature is not yet developed or when there is a real problem. Otherwise, it is a natural reaction to start ignoring specifications when they produce false negatives.

Finally, we should always end the scenario with some kind of verification. We should specify the desired outcome of actions that were performed. Following the same scenario, our Then step could be the following:

```
Then book is removed
```

This outcome strikes a balance between providing just enough data without going into design details. We could have, for example, mentioned the database or, even more specifically, MongoDB. However, in many cases, that information is not important from the behavioral point of view. We should simply confirm that the book is removed from the catalog, no matter where it is stored.

Now that we are familiar with the BDD story format, let us write the Books Store BDD story.

The Books Store BDD story

Before we start, clone the code that is available at `https://bitbucket.org/vfarcic/tdd-java-ch07-books-store`. It is an empty project that we'll use throughout this chapter. As with previous chapters, it contains branches for each section in case you miss something.

We'll write one BDD story that will be in a pure text format, in plain English and without any code. That way, all stakeholders can participate and get involved independently of their coding proficiency. Later on, we'll see how to automate the story we're writing.

Let us start by creating a new file called `administration.story` inside the stories directory:

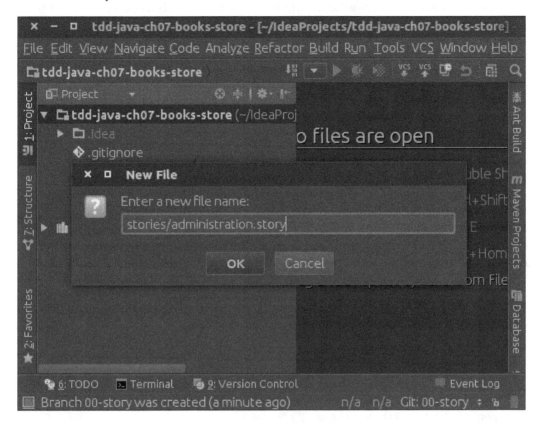

We already have the narrative that we wrote earlier, so we'll build on top of that:

```
Narrative:
In order to manage the book store collection efficiently
As a store administrator
I want to be able to add, update and remove books
```

We'll be using JBehave format for writing stories. More details regarding JBehave are coming soon. Until then, visit `http://jbehave.org/` for more info.

A narrative always starts with the `Narrative` line and is followed with the `In order to`, `As a`, and `I want to` lines. We already discussed the meaning of each of them.

Now that we know the answers to why, who, and what, it is time to sit with the rest of the team and discuss possible scenarios. We're still not talking about steps (`Given`, `When`, and `Then`), but simply what would be the outlines or short descriptions of the potential scenarios. The list could be the following:

```
Scenario: Book details form should have all fields
Scenario: User should be able to create a new book
Scenario: User should be able to display book details
Scenario: User should be able to update book details
Scenario: User should be able to delete a book
```

We're following the JBehave syntax by using `Scenario` followed by a short description. There is no reason to go into details at this stage. The purpose of this stage is to serve as a quick brainstorming session. In this case, we came up with those five scenarios. The first one should define fields of the form that we'll use to administer books. The rest of the scenarios are trying to define different administrative tasks. There's nothing truly creative about them. We're supposed to develop an MVP of a very simple application. If it proves to be successful, we can expand and truly employ our creativity. With the current objective, the application will be simple and straightforward.

Now that we know what our scenarios are; in general terms, it is time to properly define each of them. Let us start working on the first one:

```
Scenario: Book details form should have all fields

Given user is on the books screen
Then field bookId exists
Then field bookTitle exists
Then field bookAuthor exists
Then field bookDescription exists
```

This scenario does not contain any actions; there are no *When* steps. It can be considered a sanity check. It tells developers what fields should be present in the book form. Through those fields, we can decide what data schema we'll use. IDs are descriptive enough so that we know what each field is about (one ID and three text fields). Keep in mind that this scenario (and those that will follow) are pure texts without any code. The main advantage is that anyone can write them, and we'll try to keep it that way.

Let's see what the second scenario should look like:

```
Scenario: User should be able to create a new book

Given user is on the books screen
When user clicks the button newBook
When user sets values to the book form
When user clicks the button saveBook
Then book is stored
```

This scenario is a bit better formed than the previous one. There is a clear prerequisite (used should be on a certain screen); there are several actions (click on the **newBook** button, fill in the form, and click on the **saveBook** button); finally, there is the verification of the outcome (book is stored).

The rest of the scenarios are as follows (since they all work in a similar way, we feel that there is no reason to explain each of them separately):

```
Scenario: User should be able to display book details

Given user is on the books screen
When user selects a book
Then book form contains all data

Scenario: User should be able to update book details

Given user is on the books screen
When user selects a book
When user sets values to the book form
Then book is stored

Scenario: User should be able to delete a book

Given user is on the books screen
When user selects a book
When user clicks the deleteBook button
Then book is removed
```

The only thing that might be worth noticing is that we are using the same steps when appropriate (for example, When user selects a book). Since we'll soon try to automate all those scenarios, having the same text for the same step will save us some time from duplicating the code. It is important to strike the balance between the freedom to express scenarios in the best possible way and the ease of automation. There are a few more things that we can modify in our existing scenarios; however, before we refactor them, let us introduce you to JBehave.

The source code can be found in the 00-story branch of the tdd-java-ch07-books-store Git repository: https://bitbucket.org/vfarcic/tdd-java-ch07-books-store/branch/00-story.

JBehave

There are two major components required for JBehave to run BDD stories: runners and steps. A runner is a class that will parse the story, run all scenarios, and generate a report. Steps are code methods that match steps written in scenarios. The project already contains all Gradle dependencies so we can dive right into creating the JBehave runner.

JBehave runner

JBehave is no exception to the rule that every type of test needs a runner. In the previous chapters, we used JUnit and TestNG runners. While neither of those needed any special configuration, JBehave is a bit more demanding and forces us to create a class that will hold all the configuration required for running stories.

The following is the Runner code that we'll use throughout this chapter:

```
public class Runner extends JUnitStories {

    @Override
    public Configuration configuration() {
        return new MostUsefulConfiguration()
                .useStoryReporterBuilder(getReporter())
                .useStoryLoader(new LoadFromURL());
    }

    @Override
    protected List<String> storyPaths() {
        String path = "stories/**/*.story";
        return new StoryFinder().findPaths(
            CodeLocations
```

```
                    .codeLocationFromPath("")
                    .getFile(),
            Collections
                    .singletonList(path),
            new ArrayList<String>(),
            "file:"
        );
    }


    @Override
    public InjectableStepsFactory stepsFactory() {
        return new InstanceStepsFactory(
                configuration(),
                new Steps()
        );
    }


    private StoryReporterBuilder getReporter() {
        return new StoryReporterBuilder()
            .withPathResolver(
                new FilePrintStreamFactory
                        .ResolveToSimpleName()
            )
            .withDefaultFormats()
            .withFormats(Format.CONSOLE, Format.HTML);
    }


}
```

It is a very uneventful code, so we'll comment only on a few important parts. Overridden method `storyPaths` has the location to our story files set to the `stories/**/*.story` path. This is a standard Apache Ant (`http://ant.apache.org/`) syntax that, when translated to plain language, means that any file ending with `.story` inside the `stories` directory or any subdirectory (`**`) will be included. Another important overridden method is `stepsFactory`, which is used to set classes containing the steps definition (we'll work with them very soon). In this case, we set it to the instance of a single class called **Steps** (the repository already contains an empty class that we'll use later on).

The source code can be found in the 01-runner branch of the *tdd-java-ch07-books-store* Git repository: `https://bitbucket.org/vfarcic/tdd-java-ch07-books-store/branch/01-runner`.

Now that we have our runner done, it is time to fire it up and see what the result is.

Pending steps

We can run our scenarios with the following Gradle command:

```
$ gradle clean test
```

Gradle runs only tasks that changed from the last execution. Since our source code will not always change (we often modify only stories in text format), the `clean` task is required to be run before the `test` so that the cache is removed.

JBehave creates a nice report for us and puts it into the `target/jbehave/view` directory. Open the `reports.html` file in your favorite browser.

The initial page of the report displays a list of our stories (in our case, only *Administration*) and two predefined ones called **BeforeStories** and **AfterStories**. Their purpose is similar to the `@BeforeClass` and `@AfterClass` JUnit annotated methods. They are run before and after stories and can be useful for setting up and tearing down data, servers, and so on.

This initial reports page shows that we have five scenarios and all of them are in the *Pending* status. This is JBehave's way of telling us that they were neither successful nor failed, but that there is code missing behind the steps we used.

Story Reports

Stories		Scenarios				
Name	Excluded	Total	Successful	Pending	Failed	Excluded
Administration	0	5	5	5	0	0
AfterStories	0	0	0	0	0	0
BeforeStories	0	0	0	0	0	0
3	0	5	5	5	0	0

The last column in each row contains a link that allows us to see details of each story.

```
Narrative:

    In order to manage the book store collection
    As a store administrator
    I want to be able to perform insert, update and delete operations


Scenario: Book details form should have all fields

    Given user is on the books screen   (PENDING)
    Then field bookId exists   (PENDING)
    Then field bookTitle exists   (PENDING)
    Then field bookAuthor exists   (PENDING)
    Then field bookDescription exists   (PENDING)

@Given("user is on the books screen")
@Pending
public void givenUserIsOnTheBooksScreen() {
  // PENDING
}
```

In our case, all the steps are marked as pending. JBehave even puts a suggestion of a method that we need to create for each pending step.

To recapitulate, at this point, we wrote one story with five scenarios. Each of those scenarios is equivalent to a specification that will be used both as a definition that should be developed and to verify that the development was done correctly. Each of those scenarios consists of several steps that define preconditions (*Given*), actions (*When*), and the expected outcome (*Then*).

Now it is time to write the code behind our steps. However, before we start coding, let us get introduced to Selenium and Selenide.

Selenium and Selenide

Selenium is a set of drivers that can be used to automate browsers. We can use them to manipulate browsers and page elements by, for example, clicking on a button or a link, filling up a form field, opening a specific URL, and so on. There are drivers for almost any browser: Android, Chrome, FireFox, Internet Explorer, Safari, and many more. Our favorite is PhantomJS, which is a headless browser that works without any UI. Running stories with it is faster than with traditional browsers, and we often use it to get fast feedback on the readiness of web application. If it works as expected, we can proceed and try it out in all the different browsers and versions that our application is supposed to support.

More information about Selenium can be found at `http://www.seleniumhq.org/` with the list of supported drivers at `http://www.seleniumhq.org/projects/webdriver/`.

While Selenium is great for automating browsers, it has its downsides, one of them being that it is operating at a very low level. Clicking on a button, for example, is easy and can be accomplished with a single line of code:

```
selenium.click("myLink")
```

If the element with the ID `myLink` does not exist, Selenium will throw an exception and the test will fail. While we want our tests to fail when the expected element does not exist, in many cases it is not so simple. For example, our page might load dynamically with that element appearing only after an asynchronous request to the server got a response. For this reason, we might not only want to click on that element but also wait until it is available, and fail only if a timeout is reached. While this can be done with Selenium, it is tedious and error prone. Besides, why would we do the work that is already done by others? Say hello to Selenide.

Selenide (`http://selenide.org/`) is a wrapper around Selenium WebDrivers with a more concise API, support for Ajax, selectors that use JQuery style, and so on. We'll use Selenide for all our Web steps and you'll get more familiar with it soon.

Now, let us write some code.

JBehave steps

Before we start writing steps, install the PhantomJS browser. The instructions for your operating system can be found at `http://phantomjs.org/download.html`.

With `PhantomJS` installed, it is time to specify a few Gradle dependencies:

```
dependencies {
    testCompile 'junit:junit:4.+'
    testCompile 'org.jbehave:jbehave-core:3.+'
    testCompile 'com.codeborne:selenide:2.+'
    testCompile 'com.codeborne:phantomjsdriver:1.+'
}
```

You are already familiar with *JUnit* and *jbehave-core*, which was set up earlier. Two new additions are Selenide and PhantomJS. Refresh Gradle dependencies so that they are included in your IDEA project.

Now, it is time to add the PhantomJS WebDriver to our `Steps` class;

```
public class Steps {

    private WebDriver webDriver;

    @BeforeStory
    public void beforeStory() {
        if (webDriver == null) {
            webDriver = new PhantomJSDriver();
            WebDriverRunner.setWebDriver(webDriver);
            webDriver.manage().window().setSize(
                    new Dimension(1024, 768)
            );
        }
    }

}
```

We're utilizing the `@BeforeStory` annotation to define the method that we're using to do some basic setup. If a driver is not already specified, we're setting it up to be `PhantomJSDriver`. Since this application will look different on smaller devices (phones, tablets, and so on), it is important that we specify clearly what the size of the screen is. In this case, we're setting it to be a reasonable desktop/laptop monitor screen resolution of 1024 x 768.

With setup out of the way, let us code our first pending step. We can simply copy and paste the first method JBehave suggested for us in the report:

```
@Given("user is on the books screen")
public void givenUserIsOnTheBooksScreen() {
    // PENDING
}
```

Imagine that our application will have a link that will open the books screen. To do that, well need to perform two steps:

1. Open the Website home page.
2. Click on the books link in the menu.

We'll specify that this link will have the ID books. IDs are very important as they allow us to easily locate an element on the page.

The steps we described above can be translated to the following code:

```
private String url = "http://localhost:9001";

@Given("user is on the books screen")
public void givenUserIsOnTheBooksScreen() {
    open(url);
    $("#books").click();
}
```

We're assuming that our application will run on the 9001 port on the localhost. Therefore, we are first opening the home page URL and then clicking on the element with the ID books.(Selenide/JQuery syntax for specifying an ID is #).

If we run our runner again, we'd see that the first step failed and the rest is still in the *pending* state. Now, we are in the red state of the red-green-refactor cycle.

Let us continue working on the rest of the steps used in the first scenario. The second one can be the following:

```
@Then("field bookId exists")
public void thenFieldBookIdExists() {
    $("#books").shouldBe(visible);
}
```

The third one is almost the same, so we can refactor the previous method and convert an element ID into a variable:

```
@Then("field $elementId exists")
public void thenFieldExists(String elementId) {
    $("#" + elementId).shouldBe(visible);
}
```

With this change, all the steps in the first scenario are done. If we run our tests again, the result is the following:

Scenario: Book details form should have all fields

Given user is on the books screen   (FAILED)
Element not found {#books} Expected: visible Screenshot:
file:/home/vfarcic/IdeaProjects/tdd-java-ch07-books-
store/build/reports/tests/1430688921325.15.png Timeout: 4 s. Caused by:
NoSuchElementException: Error Message => 'Unable to find element with css selector
'#books"

Then field bookId exists   (NOT PERFORMED)

Then field bookTitle exists   (NOT PERFORMED)

Then field bookAuthor exists   (NOT PERFORMED)

Then field bookDescription exists   (NOT PERFORMED)

The first step failed since we did not even start working on the implementation of our Books Store application. Selenide has a nice feature, creating a screenshot of the browser every time there is a failure. We can see the path in the report. The rest of the steps are in the not performed state since the execution of the scenario stopped on failure.

What should be done next depends on the structure of the team. If the same person is working both on functional tests and the implementation, he could start working on the implementation and write just enough code to make this scenario pass. In many other situations, separate people are working on functional specification and the implementation code. In that case, one could continue working on the missing steps for the rest of the scenarios, while the other would start working on the implementation. Since all scenarios are already written in a text form, a coder already knows what should be done and the two can work in parallel. We'll take the former route and write the code for the rest of the pending steps.

Let's go through the next scenario;

> ## Scenario: User should be able to create a new book
>
> Given user is on the books screen   (FAILED)
> Element not found {#books} Expected: visible Screenshot:
> file:/home/vfarcic/IdeaProjects/tdd-java-ch07-books-
> store/build/reports/tests/1430690653894.32.png Timeout: 4 s. Caused by:
> NoSuchElementException: Error Message => 'Unable to find element with css selector
> '#books''
> When user clicks the button newBook   (NOT PERFORMED)
> When user sets values to the book form   (PENDING)
> When user clicks the button saveBook   (NOT PERFORMED)
> Then book is stored   (PENDING)

We already have half of the steps done from the previous scenario, so there are only two *pending*. After we click on the **newBook** button, we should set some values to the form, click on the **saveBook** button, and verify that the book was stored correctly. We can do the last part by checking whether it appeared in the list of available books.

The missing steps can be the following:

```
@When("user sets values to the book form")
public void whenUserSetsValuesToTheBookForm() {
    $("#bookId").setValue("123");
    $("#bookTitle").setValue("BDD Assistant");
    $("#bookAuthor").setValue("Viktor Farcic");
    $("#bookDescription").setValue(
        "Open source BDD stories editor and runner"
    );
}
@Then("book is stored")
public void thenBookIsStored() {
    $("#book123").shouldBe(present);
}
```

The second step assumes that each of the available books will have an ID in the format book[ID].

Let us take a look at the next scenario:

Scenario: User should be able to display book details

Given user is on the books screen   (FAILED)
Element not found {#books} Expected: visible Screenshot:
file:/home/vfarcic/IdeaProjects/tdd-java-ch07-books-
store/build/reports/tests/1430691141869.46.png Timeout: 4 s. Caused by:
NoSuchElementException: Error Message => 'Unable to find element with css selector
'#books''
When user selects a book   (PENDING)
Then book form contains all data   (PENDING)

Like in the previous one, there are two steps pending to be developed. We need to have a way to select a book and to verify that data in the form is correctly populated:

```
@When("user selects a book")
public void whenUserSelectsABook() {
    $("#book1").click();
}

@Then("book form contains all data")
public void thenBookFormContainsAllData() {
    $("#bookId").shouldHave(value("1"));
    $("#bookTitle").shouldHave(
        value("TDD for Java Developers")
    );
    $("#bookAuthor").shouldHave(value("Viktor Farcic"));
    $("#bookDescription").shouldHave(value("Cool book!"));
}
```

These two methods are interesting because they not only specify the expected behavior (when a specific book link is clicked, then a form with its data is displayed), but also expect certain data to be available for testing. When this scenario is run, a book with an ID 1, title `TDD for Java Developers`, author `Viktor Farcic`, and description `Cool book!` should already exist. We can choose to add that data to the database or use a mock server that will serve the predefined values. No matter what the choice of how to set test data is, we can finish with this scenario and jump into the next one.

Scenario: User should be able to update book details

Given user is on the books screen   (FAILED)
Element not found {#books} Expected: visible Screenshot:
file:/home/vfarcic/IdeaProjects/tdd-java-ch07-books-
store/build/reports/tests/1430692088078.61.png Timeout: 4 s. Caused by:
NoSuchElementException: Error Message => 'Unable to find element with css selector
'#books''

When user selects a book   (NOT PERFORMED)

When user sets new values to the book form   (PENDING)

Then book is updated   (PENDING)

The implementation of the pending steps could be the following:

```
@When("user sets new values to the book form")
public void whenUserSetsNewValuesToTheBookForm() {
    $("#bookTitle").setValue(
        "TDD for Java Developers revised"
    );
    $("#bookAuthor").setValue(
        "Viktor Farcic and Alex Garcia"
    );
    $("#bookDescription").setValue("Even better book!");
    $("#saveBook").click();
}

@Then("book is updated")
public void thenBookIsUpdated() {
    $("#book1").shouldHave(
        text("TDD for Java Developers revised")
    );
    $("#book1").click();
    $("#bookTitle").shouldHave(
```

```
        value("TDD for Java Developers revised")
    );
    $("#bookAuthor").shouldHave(
        value("Viktor Farcic and Alex Garcia")
    );
    $("#bookDescription").shouldHave(
        value("Even better book!")
    );
}
```

Finally, there is only one scenario left:

Scenario: User should be able to delete a book

Given user is on the books screen   (FAILED)
Element not found {#books} Expected: visible Screenshot:
file:/home/vfarcic/IdeaProjects/tdd-java-ch07-books-
store/build/reports/tests/1430692818420.77.png Timeout: 4 s. Caused by:
NoSuchElementException: Error Message => 'Unable to find element with css selector
'#books'

When user selects a book   (NOT PERFORMED)

When user clicks the button deleteBook   (NOT PERFORMED)

Then book is removed   (PENDING)

We can verify that a book is removed by verifying that it is not in the list of available books:

```
@Then("book is removed")
public void thenBookIsRemoved() {
    $("#book1").shouldNotBe(visible);
}
```

We're finished with the steps code. Now, the person who is developing the application not only has requirements but also has a way to validate each behavior (scenario). He can be moving through the red-green-refactor cycle one scenario at a time.

The source code can be found in the `02-steps` branch of the `tdd-java-ch07-books-store` Git repository: `https://bitbucket.org/vfarcic/tdd-java-ch07-books-store/branch/02-steps`.

Final validation

Let us imagine that a different person worked on the code that should fulfil the requirements set by our scenarios. This person picked one scenario at the time, developed the code, ran that scenario, and confirmed that his implementation was correct. Once the implementation of all scenarios has been done, it is time to run the whole story and do the final validation.

The application has been packed as a `Docker` file and we prepared a Vagrant virtual machine that will run it.

Check out the branch at `https://bitbucket.org/vfarcic/tdd-java-ch07-books-store/branch/03-validation` and run `Vagrant`:

```
$ vagrant up
```

The output should be similar to the following:

```
==> default: Importing base box 'ubuntu/trusty64'...
==> default: Matching MAC address for NAT networking...
==> default: Checking if box 'ubuntu/trusty64' is up to date...
...
==> default: Running provisioner: docker...
    default: Installing Docker (latest) onto machine...
    default: Configuring Docker to autostart containers...
==> default: Starting Docker containers...
==> default: -- Container: books-fe
```

Once Vagrant is finished, we can see the application by opening `http://localhost:9001` in our browser of choice:

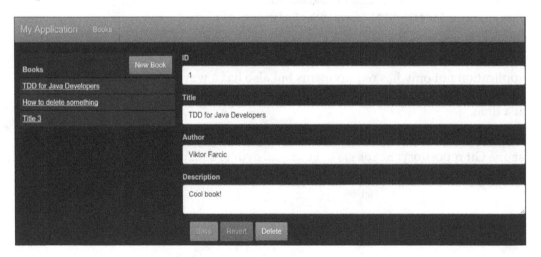

Now, let us run our scenarios again;

```
$ gradle clean test
```

This time there were no failures and all scenarios ran successfully:

Narrative:

In order to manage the book store collection
As a store administrator
I want to be able to perform insert, update and delete operations

Scenario: Book details form should have all fields

Given user is on the books screen
Then field bookId exists
Then field bookTitle exists
Then field bookAuthor exists
Then field bookDescription exists

Scenario: User should be able to create a new book

Given user is on the books screen
When user clicks the button newBook
When user sets values to the book form
When user clicks the button saveBook
Then book is stored

Once all scenarios are passing, we meet the acceptance criteria and the application can be delivered to production.

Summary

BDD, in its essence, is a flavor of TDD. It follows the same basic principle of writing tests (scenarios) before the implementation code. It drives the development and helps us better understand what should be done.

One of the major differences is the life cycle duration. While with TDD, which is based on unit tests, we're moving from red to green very fast (in minutes if not seconds); BDD often takes a higher-level approach that might require hours or days until we get from the red to the green state. Another important difference is the audience. While unit tests-based TDD is done by developers for developers, BDD intends to involve everyone through its ubiquitous language.

While a whole book can be written on this subject, our intention was to give you just enough information so that you can investigate BDD further.

Now it is time to take a look at legacy code and how to adapt it and make it more test-driven development friendly.

8

Refactoring Legacy
Code – Making it Young Again

*"Fear is the path to the dark side. Fear leads to anger. Anger leads to hate. Hate
leads to suffering."*

- Yoda

TDD might not adjust straightaway to legacy code. You may have to fiddle a bit
with the steps to make it work. Understand that your TDD might change in this case.
That, somehow, you are no longer performing the TDD you were used. This chapter
will introduce you to the world of legacy code, taking as much as we can from TDD.

We'll start a fresh, with a legacy application that is currently in production.
We'll alter it in small ways without introducing defects or regressions and
we'll even have time to have an early lunch!

The following topics are covered in this chapter:

- Legacy code
- Dealing with legacy code
- REST communication
- Dependency injection
- Tests at different levels: end to end, integration, and unit

Legacy code

Let's start with the definition of legacy code. While there are many authors with different definitions such as lack of trust in your application or your tests, code that is no longer supported, and so on, we like the one created by Michael Feathers the most:

> *Legacy code is code without tests.*
>
> *The reason for this definition is that it is objective: either there are or there aren't tests.*

> *--Michael Feathers*

How to detect legacy code? Although legacy code usually frequents bad code, Michael Feathers exposes some smells in his book *Working Effectively with Legacy* Code by *Dorling Kindersley (India) Pvt. Ltd. (1993).*

Code Smell

Smells are certain structures in the code that indicate violation of fundamental design principles and negatively impact design quality.

Code smells are usually not bugs—they are not technically incorrect and do not currently prevent the program from functioning. Instead, they indicate weaknesses in design that may be slowing down development or increasing the risk of bugs or failures in the future.

Source: `http://en.wikipedia.org/wiki/Code_smell`.

One of the common smells for legacy code is: *I can't test this code*. It is accessing outside resources, introducing other side-effects, using a new operator, and so on. In general, good design is easy to test. Let's see some legacy code.

Legacy code example

Software concepts are often easiest to explain through code and this one is no exception. We have seen and worked with the Tic-Tac-Toe application (see *Chapter 3, Red-Green-Refactor – from Failure through Success until Perfection*). The following code performs position validation:

```
public class TicTacToe {

    public void validatePosition(int x, int y) {
```

```
        if (x < 1 || x > 3) {
            throw new RuntimeException("X is outside "
                + "board");
        }
        if (y < 1 || y > 3) {
            throw new RuntimeException("Y is outside "
                + "board");
        }
    }
}
```

The specification that corresponds with this code is as follows:

```
public class TicTacToeSpec {

    @Rule
    public ExpectedException exception =
      ExpectedException.none();
    private TicTacToe ticTacToe;

    @Before
    public final void before() {
        ticTacToe = new TicTacToe();
    }

    @Test
    public void whenXOutsideBoardThenRuntimeException()
    {
        exception.expect(RuntimeException.class);
        ticTacToe.validatePosition(5, 2);
    }

    @Test
    public void whenYOutsideBoardThenRuntimeException()
    {
        exception.expect(RuntimeException.class);
        ticTacToe.validatePosition(2, 5);
    }
}
```

The JaCoCo report indicates that everything is covered (except the last line, the method's closing bracket):

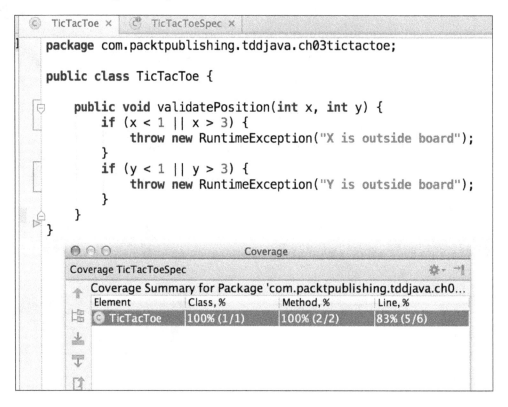

As we believe we have good coverage, we can perform an automatic and safe refactor (fragment):

```
public class TicTacToe {

    public void validatePosition(int x, int y) {
        if (isOutsideTheBoard(x)) {
            throw new RuntimeException("X is outside "
                + "board");
        }
        if (isOutsideTheBoard(y)) {
            throw new RuntimeException("Y is outside "
                + "board");
        }
    }
```

```
    private boolean isOutsideTheBoard
      (final int position) {
        return position < 1 || position > 3;
    }
}
```

This code should be ready, as the tests are successful and it has a very good test coverage.

Maybe you have already realized as much, but there is a catch. The message in the RuntimeException block is not checked for correctness; even the code coverage shows it as "covered all the branches in that line".

What is coverage all about?

Coverage is a measure used to describe the degree to which the source code of a program is tested by a particular test suite. Source: http:// en.wikipedia.org/wiki/Code_coverage.

Let's imagine a single end-to-end test that covers an easy part of the code. This test will get you a high coverage percentage, but not much security, as there are many other parts that are still not covered.

We have already introduced legacy code in our codebase: the exception messages. There might be nothing wrong with this as long as this is not an expected behavior: no one should depend on exception messages, not programmers to debug their programs, or logs, or even users. Those parts of the program that are not covered by tests are likely to suffer regressions in the near future. This might be fine if you accept the risk. Maybe the exception type and the line number are enough.

We have decided to remove the exception message, as it is not tested:

```
public class TicTacToe {

    public void validatePosition(int x, int y) {
        if (isOutsideTheBoard(x)) {
            throw new RuntimeException("");
        }
        if (isOutsideTheBoard(y)) {
            throw new RuntimeException("");
        }
    }
}
```

```
    private boolean isOutsideTheBoard
      (final int position) {
        return position < 1 || position > 3;
    }
}
```

Other ways to recognize legacy code

You might be familiar with some of the following common signs of
legacy applications:

- A patch on top of a patch, just like a living Frankenstein application
- Known bugs
- Changes are expensive
- Fragile
- Difficult to understand
- Old, outdated, static or, often, non-existent documentation
- Shotgun surgery
- Broken windows

Regarding the team that maintains it, these are some of the effects it produces
on them:

- **Resignation**: The people in charge of the software see a huge task in front
  of them
- **No one cares anymore**: If you already have broken windows in your system,
  it is easier to introduce new ones

As legacy code is usually more difficult than other kinds of software, you would
want your best people to work on it. However, we are often in a hurry imposed by
deadlines, with the idea of programming required functionalities as fast as possible
and ignoring the quality of the solution.

Therefore, to avoid wasting our talented developers in such a bad way, we expect a
non-legacy application to fulfill just the opposite. It should be:

- Easy to change
- Generalizable, configurable, and expansible
- Easy to deploy
- Robust
- No known defects or limitations

- Easy to teach to others/to learn from others
- Extensive suite of tests
- Self-validating
- Able to use keyhole surgery

As we have outlined some of the properties of legacy and non-legacy code, it should be easy to replace some qualities with others. Right? Stop shotgun surgery and use keyhole surgery, a few more details and you are done. Isn't that right?

It is not as easy as it sounds. Luckily there are some tricks and rules that, when applied, improve our code and the application comes closer to a non-legacy one.

A lack of dependency injection

This is one of the smells often detected in a legacy codebase. As there is no need to test the classes in isolation, the collaborators are instantiated where they are needed, putting the responsibility of creating collaborators and using them in the same class.

An example, using the `new` operator:

```
public class BirthdayGreetingService {

  private final MessageSender messageSender;

  public BirthdayGreetingService() {
    messageSender = new EmailMessageSender();
  }

  public void greet(final Employee employee) {
    messageSender.send(employee.getAddress(),
    "Greetings on your birthday");
  }
}
```

In the current state, the service `BirthdayGreeting` is not unit-testable. It has the dependency to `EmailMessageSender` hardcoded in the constructor. It is not possible to replace this dependency without modifying the code-base (except for injecting objects using reflection or replacing objects on the `new` operator).

Modifying the codebase is always a source of possible regressions, so it should be done with caution. Refactoring requires tests, except when it is not possible.

The Legacy Code Dilemma
When we change code, we should have tests in place. To put tests in place, we often have to change code.

The legacy code change algorithm

When you have to make a change in a legacy code base, here is an algorithm you can use:

- Identify change points
- Find test points
- Break dependencies
- Write tests
- Make changes and refactor

Applying the legacy code change algorithm

In order to apply this algorithm, we usually start with a suite of tests and always keep it green while refactoring. This is different from the normal cycle of TDD because refactoring should not introduce any new feature (that is, it should not write any new specifications).

In order to better explain the algorithm, imagine that we received the following change request:

To greet my employees in a more informal way, I want to send them a tweet instead of an email.

Identifying change points

The system is only able to send emails right now, so a change is necessary. Where? A quick investigation shows that the strategy for sending the greeting is decided in the constructor for the `BirthdayGreetingService` class following the strategy pattern `https://en.wikipedia.org/?title=Strategy_pattern` (fragment):

```
public class BirthdayGreetingService {

  public BirthdayGreetingService() {
    messageSender = new EmailMessageSender();
  }
  [...]
}
```

Finding test points

As the `BirthdayGreetingService` class does not have any collaborator injected that could be used to attach additional responsibilities to the object, the only option is to go outside this service class to test it. An option would be to change the `EmailMessageSender` class for a mock or fake implementation, but this would risk the implementation in that class.

Another option is to create an end-to-end test for this functionality:

```
public class EndToEndTest {

    @Test
    public void email_an_employee() {
        final StringBuilder systemOutput =
            injectSystemOutput();
        final Employee john = new Employee(
            new Email("john@example.com"));

        new BirthdayGreetingService().greet(john);

        assertThat(systemOutput.toString(),
            equalTo("Sent email to "
                + "'john@example.com' with "
        + "the body 'Greetings on your "
                + "birthday'\n"));
    }

    // This code has been used with permission from
    //GMaur's LegacyUtils:
    // https://github.com/GMaur/legacyutils
    private StringBuilder injectSystemOutput() {
        final StringBuilder stringBuilder =
            new StringBuilder();
        final PrintStream outputPrintStream =
            new PrintStream(
    new OutputStream() {
            @Override
            public void write(final int b)
              throws IOException {
              stringBuilder.append((char) b);
            }
        });
        System.setOut(outputPrintStream);
        return stringBuilder;
    }
}
```

This code has been used with permission from `https://github.com/GMaur/legacyutils`. This library helps you perform the technique of capturing the System out (`System.out`).

The name of the file does not end in *Specification* (or Spec), such as *TicTacToeSpec*, because this is not a specification. It is a test, to ensure the functionality remains constant. The file has been named `EndToEndTest` because we try to cover as much functionality as possible.

Breaking dependencies

After having created a test that guarantees the expected behavior does not change, we will break the hardcoded dependency between `BirthdayGreetingService` and `EmailMessageSender`. For this, we will use a technique called **Extract** and **Override Call**, which is first explained in Michaels Feathers' book:

```
public class BirthdayGreetingService {

  public BirthdayGreetingService() {
    messageSender = getMessageSender();
  }

  private MessageSender getMessageSender() {
    return new EmailMessageSender();
  }

[...]
```

Rerun the tests and the single test we have is green. We need to make this method protected or more open to be able to override it:

```
public class BirthdayGreetingService {

  protected MessageSender getMessageSender() {
    return new EmailMessageSender();
  }

[...]
```

We create a fake in the test folder. Introducing fakes in code is a pattern that consists of creating an object that could replace an existing one with the particularity that we can control its behavior. This way, we can inject some customized fakes to achieve what we need. More information is available at `http://xunitpatterns.com/`.

In this particular case, we should create a fake service that extends the original service. The next step is to override complicated methods in order to bypass irrelevant parts of code for testing purposes:

```
public class FakeBirthdayGreetingService
extends BirthdayGreetingService {

  @Override
  protected MessageSender getMessageSender() {
    return new EmailMessageSender();
  }
}
```

Now we can use the fake, instead of the `BirthdayGreetingService` class:

```
public class EndToEndTest {

  @Test
  public void email_an_employee() {
    final StringBuilder systemOutput =
      injectSystemOutput();
    final Employee john = new Employee(
      new Email("john@example.com"));

    new FakeBirthdayGreetingService().greet(john);

    assertThat(systemOutput.toString(),
      equalTo("Sent email to "
        + "'john@example.com' with "
        + "the body 'Greetings on "
        + "your birthday'\n"));
  }
```

The test is still green.

We can now apply another dependency-breaking technique "Parameterize Constructor", explained in Feathers' paper `http://www.objectmentor.com/resources/articles/WorkingEffectivelyWithLegacyCode.pdf`. The production code may look like this:

```
public class BirthdayGreetingService {

  public BirthdayGreetingService(final MessageSender
    messageSender) {
```

```
        this.messageSender = messageSender;
    }
    [...]
}
```

Test code that corresponds to this implementation can be as follows:

```
public class EndToEndTest {

  @Test
  public void email_an_employee() {
    final StringBuilder systemOutput =
      injectSystemOutput();
    final Employee john = new Employee(
      new Email("john@example.com"));

    new BirthdayGreetingService(new
        EmailMessageSender()).greet(john);

    assertThat(systemOutput.toString(),
      equalTo("Sent email to "
        + "'john@example.com' with "
        + "the body 'Greetings on "
        + "your birthday'\n"));
  }
  [...]
```

We can also remove `FakeBirthday`, as it is no longer used.

Writing tests

While keeping the old end-to-end test, create an interaction to verify the integration of `BirthdayGreetingService` and `MessageSender`:

```
  @Test
  public void the_service_should_ask_the_messageSender() {
    final Email address =
      new Email("john@example.com");
    final Employee john = new Employee(address);
    final MessageSender messageSender =
      mock(MessageSender.class);

    new BirthdayGreetingService(messageSender)
      .greet(john);

    verify(messageSender).send(address,
        "Greetings on your birthday");
  }
```

At this point, a new `TweetMessageSender` can be written, thus completing the last step of the algorithm.

The Kata exercise

The only way a programmer will be able to improve is through practice. Creating programs of different types and using different technologies usually provide a programmer with new insights into software construction. Based on this idea, a Kata is an exercise that defines some requirements or fixed features to be implemented in order to achieve some goals.

The programmer is asked to implement a possible solution and then compare it with others trying to find the best. The key value of this exercise is not getting the fastest implementation but discussing decisions taken while designing the solution. In most cases, all programs created in Kata are dropped at the end.

The Kata exercise in this chapter is about a legacy system. This is a sufficiently simple program to be processed in this chapter but also complex enough to pose some difficulties.

Legacy Kata

You have been tasked to adopt a system that is already in production, a working piece of software for a book library: the Alexandria project.

The project currently lacks documentation, and the old maintainer is no longer available for discussion. So, should you accept this mission, it is going to be entirely your responsibility, as there is no one else to rely on.

Description

We have been able to recover these specification snippets from the time the original project was written:

- The Alexandria software should be able to store books and lend them to users, who have the power to return them. The user can also query the system for books, by author, book title, status, and ID.
- There is no time frame for returning the books.
- The books can also be censored as this is considered important for business reasons.
- The software should not accept new users.
- The user should be told, at any moment, which is the server's time.

Technical comments

The Alexandria is a backend project written in Java, which communicates information to the frontend using a REST API. For the purpose of this Kata exercise, the persistence has been implemented as an in-memory object, using the Fake test double explained in `http://xunitpatterns.com/Fake%20Object.html/`.

The code is available at `https://bitbucket.org/vfarcic/tdd-chapter-08/commits/branch/legacy-code`.

Adding a new feature

Until the point of adding a new feature, the legacy code might not be a disturbance to the programmers' productivity. The codebase is in a state that is worse than desired, but the production systems work without any inconveniences.

Now is the time when the problems start to appear. The **Product Owner (PO)** wants to add a new feature.

For example, as a library manager, I want to know all the history for a given book so that I can measure which books are more in demand than others.

Black-box or spike testing

As the old maintainer of the Alexandria project is no longer available for questions and there is no documentation, the black-box testing is more difficult. Thus, we decide to get to know the software better through investigation and then doing some spikes that will leak internal knowledge to us about the system.

We will later use this knowledge to implement the new feature.

Black-box testing is a method of software testing that examines the functionality of an application without peering into its internal structures or workings. This type of test can be applied to virtually every level of software testing: unit, integration, system, and acceptance. It typically comprises most if not all higher-level testing, but can dominate unit testing as well.

Source: `http://en.wikipedia.org/wiki/Black-box_testing`.

More information on black-box testing can be found here: `http://agile.csc.ncsu.edu/SEMaterials/BlackBox.pdf`

Preliminary investigation

When we know the required feature, we will start looking at the Alexandria project:

- 15 files
- maven-based (`pom.xml`)
- 0 tests

Firstly, we want to confirm is that this project has never been tested, and the lack of a test folder reveals so:

```
$ find src/test
find: src/test: No such file or directory
```

These are the folder contents for the Java part:

```
$ cd src/main/java/com/packtpublishing/tddjava/ch08/alexandria/
$ find .
.
./Book.java
./Books.java
./BooksEndpoint.java
./BooksRepository.java
./CustomExceptionMapper.java
./MyApplication.java
./States.java
./User.java
./UserRepository.java
./Users.java
```

The rest:

```
$ cd src/main
$ find resources webapp
resources
resources/applicationContext.xml
webapp
webapp/WEB-INF
webapp/WEB-INF/web.xml
```

This seems to be a web project (indicated by the `web.xml` file), using Spring (indicated by the `applicationContext.xml`). The dependencies in the `pom.xml` show the following (fragment):

```
<dependency>
    <groupId>org.springframework</groupId>
    <artifactId>spring-web</artifactId>
    <version>4.1.4.RELEASE</version>
</dependency>
```

Having Spring is already a good sign, as it can help with the dependency injection, but a quick look showed that the context is not really being used. Maybe something that was used in the past?

In the `web.xml` file, we can find this fragment:

```
<?xml version="1.0" encoding="UTF-8"?>
<web-app version="3.0" xmlns="http://java.sun.com/xml/ns/javaee"
         xmlns:xsi="http://www.w3.org/2001/XMLSchema-instance"
         xsi:schemaLocation="http://java.sun.com/xml/ns/javaee
         http://java.sun.com/xml/ns/javaee/web-app_3_0.xsd">

    <module-name>alexandria</module-name>

    <context-param>
        <param-name>contextConfigLocation</param-name>
        <param-value>classpath:applicationContext.xml</param-value>
    </context-param>

    <servlet>
        <servlet-name>SpringApplication</servlet-name>
        <servlet-class>
org.glassfish.jersey.servlet.ServletContainer</servlet-class>
        <init-param>
            <param-name>javax.ws.rs.Application</param-name>
            <param-value>com.packtpublishing.tddjava.ch08.alexandria.
MyApplication</param-value>
        </init-param>
        <load-on-startup>1</load-on-startup>
    </servlet>
```

In this file:

- The context in `applicationContext.xml` will be loaded

- There is an application file (`com.packtpublishing.tddjava.ch08.alexandria.MyApplication`) that will be executed inside a servlet

The `MyApplication` file is as follows:

```
public class MyApplication extends ResourceConfig {

    public MyApplication() {
        register(RequestContextFilter.class);
        register(BooksEndpoint.class);
        register(JacksonJaxbJsonProvider.class);
        register(CustomExceptionMapper.class);
    }
}
```

This configures the necessary classes for executing the endpoint `BooksEndpoint` (fragment):

```
@Path("books")
@Component
public class BooksEndpoint {

    private BooksRepository books = new BooksRepository();

    private UserRepository users = new UserRepository();
```

In this last snippet, we can find one of the first indicators that this is a legacy codebase: both dependencies (`books` and `users`) are created inside the endpoint and not injected. This makes unit testing more difficult.

We can start by writing down the element that will be used during refactoring; we write the code for the dependency injection in `BooksEndpoint`.

How to find candidates for refactoring

There are different paradigms of programming (for example, functional, imperative, and object-oriented) and styles (for example, compact, verbose, minimalistic, and too-clever). Therefore, the candidates for refactoring are different from one person to the other.

There is another way, as opposed to subjectively, of finding candidates for refactoring: objectively. Research papers investigating ways of finding these ways include:

Source: http://www.bth.se/fou/cuppsats.nsf/all/2e48c5bc1c234d0ec1257c77 003ac842/$file/BTH2014SIVERLAND.pdf

Introducing the new feature

After getting to know the code more, it seems that the most important functional change is to replace the current status (fragment):

```
@XmlRootElement
public class Book {

    private final String title;
    private final String author;
    private int status; //<- this attribute
    private int id;
```

with a collection of them (fragment):

```
@XmlRootElement
public class Book {
    private int[] statuses;
    // ...
```

This might seem to work (after changing all access to the field to the array, for example), but this also prompts a functional requirement.

The Alexandria software should be able to store books and lend them to users who have the power to return them. The user can also query the system for books, by author, book title, status, and ID.

The **Product Owner (PO)** confirms that searching books via status has now changed: now it also allows to search for any previous status.

This change is getting bigger and bigger. Whenever we feel that the time for removing this legacy code has come, we start applying the legacy code algorithm.

We have also detected a primitive obsession and feature envy smell; storing the status as int (primitive obsession) and then actuating on another object's state (feature envy). We will add this to the following to-do list:

- Dependency injection in BooksEndpoint for books
- Change status for statuses
- Remove the primitive obsession for status (optional)

Applying the legacy code algorithm

In this case, the whole middle-end works as a standalone, using in-memory persistence. The same algorithm could be used if the persistence was saved into a database, but we would require some extra code to clean and populate the database between test runs.

We'll use DbUnit. More information can be found at `http://dbunit.sourceforge.net/`.

Writing end-to-end test cases

The first step we've decided to take to ensure the behavior is maintained during the a refactoring is to write end-to-end tests. In other applications that include frontend, this could be using a higher-level tool such as Selenium/Selenide.

In our case, as the frontend is not subject to refactoring, the tool can be lower-level. We have chosen to write HTTP requests for the purpose of end-to-end tests.

These requests should be automatic and testable, and should follow all existing rules for automatic tests or specifications. As we were discovering the real application behavior while writing these tests, we have decided to write a spike in a tool called Postman. (The tool can be found here: `https://chrome.google.com/webstore/detail/postman-rest-client/fdmmgilgnpjigdojojpjoooidkmcomcm`. The product website is here: `https://www.getpostman.com/`). This is also possible with a tool called curl (`http://curl.haxx.se/`).

> **What is curl?**
> curl is a command-line tool and library for transferring data with URL syntax, supporting [...] HTTP, HTTPS, [...], HTTP POST, HTTP PUT, [...].
> What's curl used for?
> curl is used in command lines or scripts to transfer data.
> Source: `http://curl.haxx.se/`.

To do this, we decide to execute the legacy software locally with the following line:

```
mvn clean jetty:run
```

This fires up a local jetty server that processes requests. The big benefit is that deployment is done automatically and there is no need to package everything and manually deploy to an application server (for example, JBoss AS, GlassFish, Geronimo, and TomEE). This can greatly speed up the process of making changes and seeing the effects, therefore decreasing the feedback lead time. Later on, we will start the server programmatically from Java code.

We start looking for functionalities. As we discovered earlier that the `BooksEndpoint` class contains the webservice endpoint definitions, this is a good place to start looking for functionalities. They are listed below:

1. Add a new book.
2. List all the books.
3. Search for books by ID, by author, by title, and by status.
4. Prepare this book to be rented.
5. Rent this book.
6. Censor this book.
7. Uncensor the book.

We launch the server manually and start writing requests:

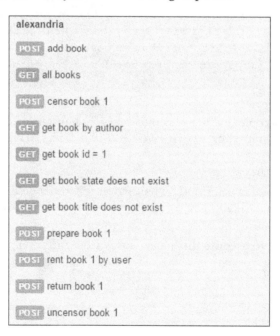

These tests seem good enough for a spike. One thing that we have realized is that each response contains a timestamp, so this makes our automation more difficult:

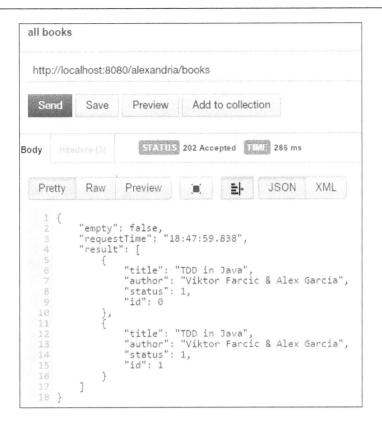

For the tests to have more value, they should be automated and exhaustive.
For the moment, they are not, so we consider them spikes. They will be
automated in the future.

Each and every single test that we perform is not automated. In this case,
the tests from the Postman interface are much faster to write than the
automated ones. Also, the experience is far more representative of what
production use would be like. The test client (thankfully, in this case)
could introduce some problems with the production one, and therefore
not return trusted results.

In this particular case, we have found that the Postman tests are a better
investment because, even after writing them, we will throw them away.
They give a very rapid feedback on the API and results. We also use
this tool for prototyping the REST APIs, as its tools are both effective
and useful.

The general idea here is: depending on whether you want to save those
tests for the future or not, use one tool or another. This also depends on
how often you want to execute them, and in which environment.

After writing down all the requests, these are the states that we have found in the application, represented by a state diagram:

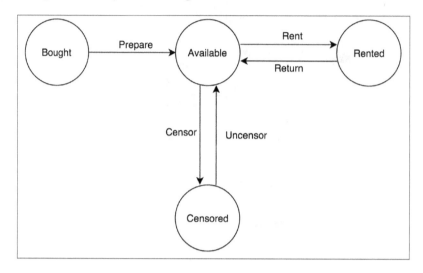

After these tests are ready and we start to understand the application, it is time to automate the tests. After all, if they are not automated, we don't really feel confident enough for refactoring.

Automating the test cases

We proceed to start the server programmatically. For this, we have decided to use Grizzly (https://grizzly.java.net/), which allows us to start the server using the configuration from Jersey's ResourceConfig (FQCN: org.glassfish.jersey. server.ResourceConfig), as shown on the test BooksEndpointTest (fragment):

The code can be found at https://bitbucket.org/vfarcic/tdd-chapter-08/ commits/branch/refactor/inject-dependencies:

```
public class BooksEndpointTest {
    public static final URI FULL_PATH =
      URI.create("http://localhost:8080/alexandria");
    private HttpServer server;

    @Before
    public void setUp() throws IOException {
        ResourceConfig resourceConfig =
          new MyApplication();
        server = GrizzlyHttpServerFactory
```

```
        .createHttpServer(FULL_PATH, resourceConfig);
      server.start();
  }

  @After
  public void tearDown(){
      server.shutdownNow();
  }
```

This prepares a local server in the address `http://localhost:8080/alexandria`. It will only be available for a short period of time (while the tests run), so if you need to manually access the server, whenever you want to pause the execution, insert a call to the following method:

```
public void pauseTheServer() throws Exception {
    System.in.read();
}
```

When you want to stop the server, stop the execution or hit Enter in the allocated console.

Now we can start the server programmatically, pause it (with the preceding method), and execute the spike again. The results are the same, therefore the refactor is successful.

We add the first automated test to the system:

The code can be found at `https://bitbucket.org/vfarcic/tdd-chapter-08/commits/branch/refactor/inject-dependencies`:

```
public class BooksEndpointTest {

    public static final String AUTHOR_BOOK_1 =
      "Viktor Farcic and Alex Garcia";
    public static final String TITLE_BOOK_1 =
      "TDD in Java";
    private final Map<String, String> TDD_IN_JAVA;

    public BooksEndpointTest() {
        TDD_IN_JAVA = getBookProperties(TITLE_BOOK_1,
AUTHOR_BOOK_1);
    }

    private Map<String, String> getBookProperties
      (String title, String author) {
```

```java
        Map<String, String> bookProperties =
            new HashMap<>();
        bookProperties.put("title", title);
        bookProperties.put("author", author);
        return bookProperties;
    }

    @Test
    public void add_one_book() throws IOException {
        final Response books1 = addBook(TDD_IN_JAVA);
        assertBooksSize(books1, is("1"));
    }

     private void assertBooksSize(Response response,
        Matcher<String> matcher) {
        response.then().body(matcher);
    }

    private Response addBook
        (Map<String, ?> bookProperties) {
        return RestAssured
            .given().log().path()
            .contentType(ContentType.URLENC)
            .parameters(bookProperties)
            .post("books");
    }
```

For testing purposes, we're using a library called RestAssured (`https://code.google.com/p/rest-assured/`) that allows for easier testing of REST and JSON.

To complete the automated test suite, we create these tests:

1. `add_one_book()`.
2. `add_a_second_book()`.
3. `get_book_details_by_id()`.
4. `get_several_books_in_a_row()`.
5. `censor_a_book()`.
6. `cannot_retrieve_a_censored_book()`.

The code is found in `https://bitbucket.org/vfarcic/tdd-chapter-08/commits/branch/refactor/inject-dependencies`:

Now that we have a suite that ensures that no regression is introduced, we take a look at the following to-do list:

1. Dependency injection in BooksEndpoint for books.

2. Change status for statuses.

3. Remove the primitive obsession for status (optional).

We will tackle the dependency injection first.

Injecting the BookRepository dependency

The creation of the `BookRepository` dependency is in `BooksEndpoint` (fragment):

```
@Path("books")
@Component
public class BooksEndpoint {

    private BooksRepository books =
       new BooksRepository();
    [...]
```

Extract and override call

We will apply the already introduced refactoring technique "extract and override call". For this, we create a failing specification, as shown here:

```
@Test
public void add_one_book() throws IOException {
    addBook(TDD_IN_JAVA);

    Book tddInJava = new Book(TITLE_BOOK_1,
      AUTHOR_BOOK_1,
        States.fromValue(1));

    verify(booksRepository).add(tddInJava);
}
```

To pass this red specification, also known as a failing specificiation, we will first extract the dependency creation to a protected method in `BookRepository` class:

```
@Path("books")
@Component
public class BooksEndpoint {
```

```
    private BooksRepository books =
      getBooksRepository();

  [...]

   protected BooksRepository
     getBooksRepository() {
       return new BooksRepository();
  }

  [...]
```

We copy the `MyApplication` launcher to this:

```
public class TestApplication
    extends ResourceConfig {

    public TestApplication
      (BooksEndpoint booksEndpoint) {
        register(booksEndpoint);
        register(RequestContextFilter.class);
        register(JacksonJaxbJsonProvider.class);
        register(CustomExceptionMapper.class);
    }

    public TestApplication() {
        this(new BooksEndpoint(
          new BooksRepository()));
    }
}
```

This allows us to inject any `BooksEndpoint`. In this case, in the test `BooksEndpointInteractionTest`, we will override the dependency getter with a mock. In this way, we can check that the necessary calls are being made (fragment from `BooksEndpointInteractionTest`):

```
@Test
public void add_one_book() throws IOException {
    addBook(TDD_IN_JAVA);
    verify(booksRepository)
      .add(new Book(TITLE_BOOK_1,
          AUTHOR_BOOK_1, 1));
}
```

Run the tests; everything is green. Even though the specifications are successful, we have introduced a piece of design only for test purposes, and the production code is not executing this new launcher `TestApplication` but is still executing the old `MyApplication`. To solve this this, we have to unify both launchers into one. This can be solved with the refactor "Parametrize constructor", also explained in Roy Osherove's book "The Art of Unit Testing" (`http://artofunittesting.com`).

Parameterizing a constructor

We can unify the launchers accepting a `BooksEndpoint` dependency: if we don't specify it, it will register the dependency with the real instance of `BooksRepository`. Otherwise, it will register the received one:

```java
public class MyApplication
    extends ResourceConfig {

    public MyApplication() {
        this(new BooksEndpoint(
            new BooksRepository()));
    }

    public MyApplication
      (BooksEndpoint booksEndpoint) {
        register(booksEndpoint);
        register(RequestContextFilter.class);
        register(JacksonJaxbJsonProvider.class);
        register(CustomExceptionMapper.class);
    }
}
```

In this case, we have opted for 'constructor chaining' to avoid repetition in the constructors.

After doing this refactor, the `BooksEndpointInteractionTest` class is as follows, in its final state:

```java
public class BooksEndpointInteractionTest {

    public static final URI FULL_PATH = URI.
        create("http://localhost:8080/alexandria");
    private HttpServer server;
    private BooksRepository booksRepository;

    @Before
    public void setUp() throws IOException {
        booksRepository = mock(BooksRepository.class);
```

```
        BooksEndpoint booksEndpoint =
          new BooksEndpoint(booksRepository);
        ResourceConfig resourceConfig =
          new MyApplication(booksEndpoint);
        server = GrizzlyHttpServerFactory
            .createHttpServer(FULL_PATH, resourceConfig);
        server.start();
    }
```

The first test passed, so we can mark the dependency injection task as done.

The to-do list:

- Dependency injection in BooksEndpoint for books
- Change status for statuses
- Remove the primitive obsession for status (optional)

Adding a new feature

Once we have the necessary test environment in place, we can add the new feature.

As a library manager, I want to know all the history for a given book so that I can measure which books are more in demand than others.

We will start with a red specification:

```
public class BooksSpec {

    @Test
    public void should_search_for_any_past_state() {
        Book book1 = new Book("title", "author",
          States.AVAILABLE);
        book1.censor();

        Books books = new Books();
        books.add(book1);

        String available =
          String.valueOf(States.AVAILABLE);
        assertThat(
          books.filterByState(available).isEmpty(),
          is(false));
    }
}
```

Run all the tests and see the last one fail.

Implement the search on all states (fragment):

```java
public class Book {

    private ArrayList<Integer> status;

    public Book(String title, String author, int status) {
        this.title = title;
        this.author = author;
        this.status = new ArrayList<>();
        this.status.add(status);
    }

    public int getStatus() {
        return status.get(status.size()-1);
    }

    public void rent() {
        status.add(States.RENTED);
    }
    [...]

    public List<Integer> anyState() {
        return status;
    }
    [...]
```

In this fragment, we have omitted the irrelevant parts: things that were not modified or more modifier methods such as `rent` that have changed the implementation in the same fashion:

```java
public class Books {
    public Books filterByState(String state) {
        Integer expectedState = Integer.valueOf(state);
        return new Books(
            new ConcurrentLinkedQueue<>(
                books.stream()
                    .filter(x
                -> x.anyState()
                    .contains(expectedState))
                    .collect(toList()))));
    }
    [...]
```

The outside methods, especially the serialization to JSON, are not affected as the method `getStatus` still returns an `int` value.

We run all the tests and everything is green.

The to-do list:

- Dependency injection in BooksEndpoint for books
- Change status for statuses
- Remove the primitive obsession for status (optional)

Removing the primitive obsession with status as Int

We have decided to also tackle the optional item in our to-do list.

The to-do list:

- Dependency injection in BooksEndpoint for books
- Change status for statuses
- Remove the primitive obsession for status (optional)

> The Smell: Primitive Obsession involves using primitive data types to represent domain ideas. For example, we use a string to represent a message, an integer to represent an amount of money, or a Struct/Dictionary/Hash to represent a specific object.
>
> The source is: `http://c2.com/cgi/wiki?PrimitiveObsession`.

As this is a refactor step (that is, we are not introducing any new behavior into the system), we don't need any new specification. We will proceed and try to always stay green or leave it for as little time as possible.

We have converted the `States` from a `java` class with constants:

```
public class States {
    public static final int BOUGHT = 1;
    public static final int RENTED = 2;
    public static final int AVAILABLE = 3;
    public static final int CENSORED = 4;
}
```

to an enum:

```
enum States {
    BOUGHT (1),
    RENTED (2),
    AVAILABLE (3),
    CENSORED (4);

    private final int value;

    private States(int value) {
        this.value = value;
    }

    public int getValue() {
        return value;
    }

    public static States fromValue(int value) {
        for (States states : values()) {
            if(states.getValue() == value) {
                return states;
            }
        }
        throw new IllegalArgumentException(
          "Value '" + value
+ "' could not be found in States");
    }
}
```

Adapt the tests as follows:

```
public class BooksEndpointInteractionTest {
    @Test
    public void add_one_book() throws IOException {
        addBook(TDD_IN_JAVA);
        verify(booksRepository).add(
            new Book(TITLE_BOOK_1, AUTHOR_BOOK_1,
              States.BOUGHT));
    }
    [...]
public class BooksTest {
```

```
@Test
public void should_search_for_any_past_state() {
    Book book1 = new Book("title", "author",
      States.AVAILABLE);
    book1.censor();

    Books books = new Books();
    books.add(book1);

    assertThat(books.filterByState(
        String.valueOf(
          States.AVAILABLE.getValue())))
        .isEmpty(), is(false));
}
[...]
```

Adapt the production code. The code snippet is as follows:

```
@XmlRootElement
public class Books {
    public Books filterByState(String state) {
      State expected =
        States.fromValue(Integer.valueOf(state));
      return new Books(
          new ConcurrentLinkedQueue<>(
              books.stream()
                .filter(x -> x.anyState()
                  .contains(expected))
                .collect(toList()))));
}
[...]
```

Also the following:

```
@XmlRootElement
public class Book {

    private final String title;
    private final String author;
    @XmlTransient
    private ArrayList<States> status;
    private int id;
```

```
public Book
  (String title, String author, States status) {
    this.title = title;
    this.author = author;
    this.status = new ArrayList<>();
    this.status.add(status);
}

public States getStatus() {
    return status.get(status.size() - 1);
}

@XmlElement(name = "status")
public int getStatusAsInteger(){
    return getStatus().getValue();
}

public List<States> anyState() {
    return status;
}
[...]
```

In this case, the serialization has been done using the annotation:

```
@XmlElement(name = "status")
```

This converts the result of the method into the field named `status`.

Also, the field `status`, now `ArrayList<States>`, is marked with `@XmlTransient` so it is not serialized to JSON.

We execute all the tests and they are green, so we can now cross off the optional element in our to-do list:

The to-do list:

- Dependency injection in `BooksEndpoint` for books
- Change status for statuses
- Remove the primitive obsession for status (optional)

Summary

As you already know, inheriting a legacy codebase might be a daunting task.

We stated that legacy code is code without tests, so the first step in dealing with it is to create tests to help you preserve the same functionality during the process. Unfortunately, creating tests is not always as easy as it sounds. Many times, legacy code is tightly coupled and presents other symptoms that show a poor design or at least a lack of interest in the code's quality in the past. Worry not, you can perform some of the tedious tasks step by step, as shown in `http://martinfowler.com/bliki/ParallelChange.html`. Moreover, it is also well known that software development is a learning process. Working code is a side-effect. Therefore, the most important part is to learn more about the codebase, to be able to modify it with security. Please visit `http://www.slideshare.net/ziobrando/model-storming` for more information.

Finally, we encourage you to read Michael Feathers' book called *Working Effectively with Legacy Code*. It has plenty of techniques for this kind of codebase and as a result is very helpful in understanding the whole process.

9
Feature Toggles – Deploying Partially Done Features to Production

"Do not let circumstances control you. You change your circumstances."

– Jackie Chan

We have seen so far how TDD makes the development process easier and decreases the amount of time spent on writing quality code. But, there's another particular benefit to this. As code is being tested and its correctness is widely proven: we can go a step further and assume that our code is production-ready once all tests are passed.

There are some software life cycle approaches based on this idea. Some eXtreme Programming practices such as **Continuous Integration**, **Continuous Delivery**, and **Continuous Deployment** will be introduced.

The following topics will be covered in this chapter:

- Continuous Integration, Delivery, and Deployment
- Testing the application in production
- Feature Toggles

Continuous Integration, Delivery, and Deployment

Test-driven development goes hand in hand with **Continuous Integration (CI)**, **Delivery**, or **Deployment (CD)**. Differences aside, all three techniques have similar goals. They are all trying to foster continuous verification of production readiness of our code. In that aspect, they are very similar to TDD. They both promote very short development cycles, continuous verification of the code we're producing, and the intention to keep our application continuously in production-ready state.

The scope of this book does not permit us to go into the details of those techniques. Indeed, a whole book could be written on this subject. We'll just briefly explain the differences between the three. Practicing Continuous Integration means that our code is at (almost) all times integrated with the rest of the system and if there is a problem, it will surface quickly. If such a thing happens, the priority is to fix the cause of that problem, meaning that any new development must take lower priority. You might have noticed a similarity between this definition and the way TDD works. The major difference is that with TDD, our primary focus is not the integration with the rest of the system. The rest is the same. Both TDD and Continuous Integration try to detect problems fast and treat fixing them as the highest priority, putting everything else on hold. Continuous Integration does not have the whole pipeline automated, and additional manual verifications are needed before the code is deployed to production.

Continuous Delivery is very similar to Continuous Integration, except that the former goes a bit further and has the whole pipeline automated except the actual deployment to production. Every push to the repository that passed all verifications is considered valid for deployment to production. However, the decision to deploy is made manually. Someone needs to choose one of the builds and promote it to the production environment. The choice is political or functional. It depends on what and when we want our users to receive, even though each is production-ready.

> *"Continuous Delivery is a software development discipline where you build software in such a way that the software can be released to production at any time."*
>
> *– Martin Fowler*

Finally, Continuous Deployment is accomplished when the decision about what to deploy is automated as well. In this scenario, every commit that passed all verifications is deployed to production—no exceptions.

In order to continuously integrate or deliver our code to production, branches cannot exist, or the time between creating them and integrating them with the mainline must be very short (less than a day, preferably a few hours). If that is not the case, we are not continuously verifying our code.

The true connection with TDD comes from the necessity to create validations before the code is committed. If those verifications are not created in advance, code pushed to the repository is not accompanied with tests and the process fails. Without tests, there is no confidence in what we did. Without TDD, there are no tests to accompany our implementation code. Alternatively, delay pushing commits to repository until tests are created; but, in that case, there is no *Continuous* part of the process. Code is sitting on someone's computer until someone else is finished with tests. Code that sits somewhere is not continuously verified against the whole system.

To summarize, Continuous Integration, Delivery, or Deployment rely on tests to accompany the integration code (thus, relying on TDD) and on the practice of not using branches or having them very short-lived (merged to the mainline very often). The problem is with the fact that some features cannot be developed that fast. No matter how small our features are, in some cases, it might take days to develop them. During all that time, we cannot push to repository because the process would deliver them to production. Users do not want to see partial features. There is no point having, for example, part of the login process delivered. If one were to see a login page with a username, password, and login button, but the process behind that button does not actually store that info and provides, let's say, an authentication cookie, then at best we would have confused the users. In some other cases, one feature cannot work without the other. Following the same example, even if a login feature is fully developed without registration, it is pointless. One cannot be used without the other.

Imagine playing a puzzle. We need to have a rough idea of the final picture, but we are focused on one piece at the time. We pick a piece that we think is the easiest to place and combine it with it's neighbors. Only when all of them are in place is the picture complete and we are finished.

The same applies to TDD. We develop our code by being focused on small units. As we progress, they start getting a shape and working with each other until they are all integrated. While we're waiting for that to happen, even though all our tests are passing and we are in a green state, the code is not ready for the end users.

The easiest way to solve those problems and not compromise on TDD and CI/CD is to use Feature Toggles.

Feature Toggles

You might have also heard about this as Feature Flipping or Feature Flags. No matter which expression we use, they are all based on a mechanism that permits you to turn on and off the features of your application. This is very useful when all code is merged into one branch, and you must deal with partially finished (or integrated) code. With this technique, unfinished features can be hidden so users cannot access them.

Due to its nature, there are other possible uses for this functionality. As a circuit breaker when something is wrong with a particular feature, providing graceful degradation of the application, shutting down secondary features to preserve hardware resources for business core operations, and so on. Feature Toggles, in some cases, can go even further. We might use them to enable features only to certain users based on, for example, geographic location or their role. Another useful usage is that we can enable new features only for our testers. That way, end users would continue to be oblivious of the existence of some new features, while testers would be able to validate them on a production server.

Moreover, there are some aspects to remember when using Feature Toggle:

- Use toggles only until they are fully deployed and proven to work. Otherwise, you might end up with `spaghetti` code full of if/else statements containing old toggles that are not in use any more.

- Do not spend too much time testing toggles. It is, in most cases, enough to confirm that the entry point into some new feature is not visible. That can be, for example, a link to that new feature.

- Do not overuse toggles. Do not use them when there is no need for them. For example, you might be developing a new screen that is accessible through the link in the home page. If that link is added at the end, there might be no need to have a toggle that hides it.

There are many good frameworks and libraries for application feature handling. Two of them are the following:

- Togglz (`http://www.togglz.org/`)
- FF4J (`http://ff4j.org/`)

These libraries offer a sophisticated way to manage features, even adding role-based or rules-based feature access. In many cases you aren't going to need it, but these capabilities bring us the possibility of testing a new feature in production without opening it to all users. However, implementing by ourselves a custom basic solution for feature toggling is quite simple, and we are going to go through an example to illustrate this.

A Feature Toggle example

Here we go with our demo application. This time, we're going to build a simple and small **REST** service to compute on demand a concrete Nth position of Fibonacci's sequence. We will keep track of enabled/disabled features using a file. For simplicity, we will use **spring-boot** as our framework of choice and **Thymeleaf** as a template engine. This is also included in the spring-boot dependency. Find more information about spring-boot and related projects at http://projects.spring.io/spring-boot/. Also, you can visit http://www.thymeleaf.org/ to read more about the template engine.

This is how the `build.gradle` file looks like:

```
apply plugin: 'java'
apply plugin: 'application'

sourceCompatibility = 1.8
version = '1.0'
mainClassName = "com.packtpublishing.tddjava.ch09.Application"

repositories {
    mavenLocal()
    mavenCentral()
}

dependencies {
    compile group: 'org.springframework.boot',
            name: 'spring-boot-starter-thymeleaf',
            version: '1.2.4.RELEASE'

    testCompile group: 'junit',
    name: 'junit',
    version: '4.12'
}
```

Note that `application plugin` is present because we want to run the application using the Gradle command run. Here is the application's main class:

```
@SpringBootApplication
public class Application {
    public static void main(String[] args) {
        SpringApplication.run(Application.class, args);
    }
}
```

We will create the properties file. This time, we are going to use YAML format, as it is very comprehensive and concise. Add a file called `application.yml` in the `src/main/resources` folder with the following content:

```
features:
    fibonacci:
        restEnabled: false
```

Spring offers a way to load this kind of property file automatically. Currently, there are only two restrictions: the name must be `application.yml` and/or the file should be included in the application's class path.

This is our implementation of the features `config` file:

```
@Configuration
@EnableConfigurationProperties
@ConfigurationProperties(prefix = "features.fibonacci")
public class FibonacciFeatureConfig {
    private boolean restEnabled;

    public boolean isRestEnabled() {
        return restEnabled;
    }

    public void setRestEnabled(boolean restEnabled) {
        this.restEnabled = restEnabled;
    }
}
```

This is the `fibonacci` service class. This time, the computation operation will always return `-1`, just to simulate a partially done feature:

```
@Service("fibonacci")
public class FibonacciService {

    public int getNthNumber(int n) {
        return -1;
    }
}
```

We also need a wrapper to hold the computed values;

```
public class FibonacciNumber {
    private final int number, value;

    public FibonacciNumber(int number, int value) {
```

```
        this.number = number;
        this.value = value;
    }

    public int getNumber() {
        return number;
    }

    public int getValue() {
        return value;
    }
}
```

This is the `fibonacciRESTController` class, responsible for handling the `fibonacci` service queries:

```
@RestController
public class FibonacciRestController {
    @Autowired
    FibonacciFeatureConfig fibonacciFeatureConfig;

    @Autowired
    @Qualifier("fibonacci")
    private FibonacciService fibonacciProvider;

    @RequestMapping(value = "/fibonacci", method = GET)
    public FibonacciNumber fibonacci(
            @RequestParam(
                    value = "number",
                    defaultValue = "0") int number) {
        if (fibonacciFeatureConfig.isRestEnabled()) {
            int fibonacciValue = fibonacciProvider
                    .getNthNumber(number);
            return new FibonacciNumber(number, fibonacciValue);
        } else throw new UnsupportedOperationException();
    }

    @ExceptionHandler(UnsupportedOperationException.class)
    public void unsupportedException(HttpServletResponse response)
            throws IOException {
        response.sendError(
                HttpStatus.SERVICE_UNAVAILABLE.value(),
                "This feature is currently unavailable"
        );
```

```
        }

        @ExceptionHandler(Exception.class)
        public void handleGenericException(
                HttpServletResponse response,
                Exception e) throws IOException {
            String msg = "There was an error processing " +
                    "your request: " + e.getMessage();
            response.sendError(
                    HttpStatus.BAD_REQUEST.value(),
                    msg
            );
        }
    }
```

Note that the `fibonacci` method is checking whether the `fibonacci` service should be enabled or disabled, throwing an `UnsupportedOperationException` for convenience in the last case. There are also two error-handling functions; the first one is for processing `UnsupportedOperationException` and the second is for generic exceptions handling.

Now that all the components have been set, all we need to do is execute Gradle's run command:

```
$> gradle run
```

The command will launch a process that will eventually set a server up on the following address: `http://localhost:8080`. This can be observed in the console output:

```
...

2015-06-19 03:44:54.157  INFO 3886 --- [            main] o.s.w.s.handler.
SimpleUrlHandlerMapping  : Mapped URL path [/webjars/**] onto
handler of type [class org.springframework.web.servlet.resource.
ResourceHttpRequestHandler]

2015-06-19 03:44:54.160  INFO 3886 --- [            main]
o.s.w.s.handler.SimpleUrlHandlerMapping  : Mapped URL path [/**]
onto handler of type [class org.springframework.web.servlet.resource.
ResourceHttpRequestHandler]

2015-06-19 03:44:54.319  INFO 3886 --- [            main] o.s.w.s.handler.
SimpleUrlHandlerMapping  : Mapped URL path [/**/favicon.ico] onto
handler of type [class org.springframework.web.servlet.resource.
ResourceHttpRequestHandler]
```

```
2015-06-19 03:44:54.495  INFO 3886 --- [        main] o.s.j.e.a.Annota
tionMBeanExporter        : Registering beans for JMX exposure on startup
2015-06-19 03:44:54.649  INFO 3886 --- [        main] s.b.c.e.t.Tomcat
EmbeddedServletContainer : Tomcat started on port(s): 8080 (http)
2015-06-19 03:44:54.654  INFO 3886 --- [        main] c.p.tddjava.
ch09.Application         : Started Application in 6.916 seconds (JVM
running for 8.558)
> Building 75% > :run
```

Once the application has started, we can perform a query using a regular browser. The URL of the query is `http://localhost:8080/fibonacci?number=7`.

This gives us the following output:

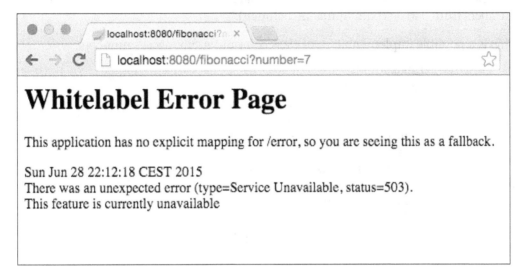

As you can see, the error received corresponds to the error sent by the REST API when the feature is disabled. Otherwise, the return should be `-1`.

Implementing the Fibonacci service

Most of you might be familiar with Fibonacci's numbers. Here's a brief explanation anyway for those who don't know what they are.

Fibonacci's sequence is an integer sequence resulting from the recurrence $f(n) = f(n-1) - f(n-2)$. The sequence starts with being $f(0) = 0$ and $f(1) = 1$.

All other numbers are generated applying the recurrence as many times as needed until a value substitution can be performed using either 0 or 1 known values.

That is: **0, 1, 1, 2, 3, 5, 8, 13, 21, 34, 55, 89, 144,...**

More info about Fibonacci's sequence can be found here: `http://www. wolframalpha.com/input/?i=fibonacci+sequence`

As an extra functionality, we want to limit how long the value computation takes so we impose a constraint on the input; our service will only compute Fibonacci's numbers from 0 to 30 (both numbers included).

This is a possible implementation of class computing Fibonacci's numbers:

```
@Service("fibonacci")
public class FibonacciService {
    public static final int LIMIT = 30;

    public int getNthNumber(int n) {
        if (isOutOfLimits(n) {
        throw new IllegalArgumentException(
        "Requested number must be a positive " +
            number no bigger than " + LIMIT);
        if (n == 0) return 0;
        if (n == 1 || n == 2) return 1;
        int first, second = 1, result = 1;
        do {
            first = second;
            second = result;
            result = first + second;
            --n;
        } while (n > 2);
        return result;
    }

    private boolean isOutOfLimits(int number) {
        return number > LIMIT || number < 0;
    }
}
```

For the sake of the brevity, TDD red-green-refactor process is not explicitly explained through the demonstration, but has been present through the development. Only the final implementation with the final tests is presented:

```java
public class FibonacciServiceTest {
    private FibonacciService tested;
    private final String expectedExceptionMessage =
        "Requested number " +
            "must be a positive number no bigger than " +
            FibonacciService.LIMIT;

    @Rule
    public ExpectedException exception = ExpectedException.none();

    @Before
    public void beforeTest() {
        tested = new FibonacciService();
    }

    @Test
    public void test0() {
        int actual = tested.getNthNumber(0);
        assertEquals(0, actual);
    }

    @Test
    public void test1() {
        int actual = tested.getNthNumber(1);
        assertEquals(1, actual);
    }

    @Test
    public void test7() {
        int actual = tested.getNthNumber(7);
        assertEquals(13, actual);
    }

    @Test
    public void testNegative() {
        exception.expect(IllegalArgumentException.class);
        exception.expectMessage(is(expectedExceptionMessage));
        tested.getNthNumber(-1);
    }
```

```
    @Test
    public void testOutOfBounce() {
        exception.expect(IllegalArgumentException.class);
        exception.expectMessage(is(expectedExceptionMessage));
        tested.getNthNumber(31);
    }
}
```

Also, we can now turn on the `fibonacci` feature in the `application.yml` file, perform some queries with the browser, and check how is it going:

```
features:
    fibonacci:
        restEnabled: true
```

Execute the Gradle's run command:

$>gradle run

Now we can fully test our REST API using the browser, with a number between 0 and 30.

With a number bigger than 30, and lastly by introducing characters instead of numbers:

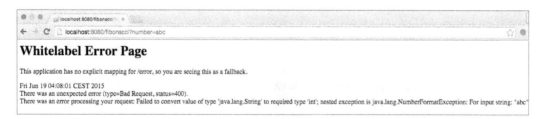

Working with the template engine

We are enabling and disabling the `fibonacci` feature, but there are many other cases where the Feature Toggle can be very useful. One of them is hiding a web link that links to an unfinished feature. This is an interesting use because we can test what we released to production using its URL, but it will be hidden for the rest of users for as long as we want.

To illustrate this behavior, we are going to create a simple web page using the already mentioned `Thymeleaf` framework.

First of all, we add a new `control` flag:

```
features:
    fibonacci:
        restEnabled: true
        webEnabled: true
```

Next, map this new flag in a configuration class:

```
private boolean webEnabled;
public boolean isWebEnabled() {
    return webEnabled;
}

public void setWebEnabled(boolean webEnabled) {
    this.webEnabled = webEnabled;
}
```

We are going to create two templates. The first one is the home page. It contains some links to different Fibonacci numbers computations. These links should be visible only when the feature is enabled, so there's an optional block to simulate this behavior:

```
<!DOCTYPE html>
<html xmlns:th="http://www.thymeleaf.org">
<head lang="en">
    <meta http-equiv="Content-Type"
            content="text/html; charset=UTF-8" />
    <title>HOME - Fibonacci</title>
</head>
<body>
<div th:if="${isWebEnabled}">
    <p>List of links:</p>
    <ul th:each="number : ${arrayOfInts}">
        <li><a
```

```
                    th:href="@{/web/fibonacci(number=${number})}"
                    th:text="'Compute ' + ${number} + 'th fibonacci'">
            </a></li>
        </ul>
    </div>
    </body>
    </html>
```

The second one just shows the value of the computed Fibonacci number and also a link to go back to the home page:

```
<!DOCTYPE html>
<html xmlns:th="http://www.thymeleaf.org">
<head lang="en">
    <meta http-equiv="Content-Type"
            content="text/html; charset=UTF-8" />
    <title>Fibonacci Example</title>
</head>
<body>
<p th:text="${number} + 'th number: ' + ${value}"></p>
<a th:href="@{/}">back</a>
</body>
</html>
```

In order to get both templates to work, they should be in a specific location. They are `src/main/resources/templates/home.html` and `src/main/resources/templates/fibonacci.html`, respectively.

Finally, the master piece, which is the controller that connects all this and makes it work:

```
@Controller
public class FibonacciWebController {
    @Autowired
    FibonacciFeatureConfig fibonacciFeatureConfig;

    @Autowired
    @Qualifier("fibonacci")
    private FibonacciService fibonacciProvider;

    @RequestMapping(value = "/", method = GET)
    public String home(Model model) {
        model.addAttribute(
            "isWebEnabled",
            fibonacciFeatureConfig.isWebEnabled()
        );
        if (fibonacciFeatureConfig.isWebEnabled()) {
            model.addAttribute(
                "arrayOfInts",
                Arrays.asList(5, 7, 8, 16)
```

```
            );
        }
        return "home";
    }

    @RequestMapping(value ="/web/fibonacci", method = GET)
    public String fibonacci(
            @RequestParam(value = "number") Integer number,
            Model model) {
        if (number != null) {
            model.addAttribute("number", number);
            model.addAttribute(
                "value",
                fibonacciProvider.getNthNumber(number));
        }
        return "fibonacci";
    }
}
```

Note that this controller and the previous one seen in the REST API example share some similarities. This is because both are constructed with the same framework and use the same resources. However, there are slight differences between them; one is annotated as @Controller instead of both being @RestController. This is because the web controller is serving template pages with custom information, while the REST API generates a JSON object response.

Let's see this working, again using the Gradle command:

$> gradle clean run

This is the generated home page:

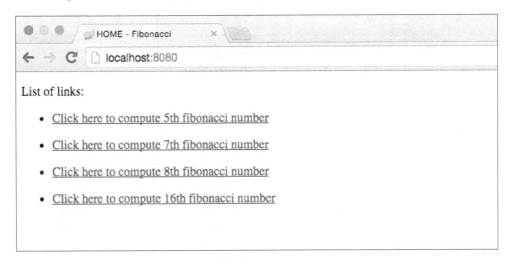

This is shown when visiting the Fibonacci's number link:

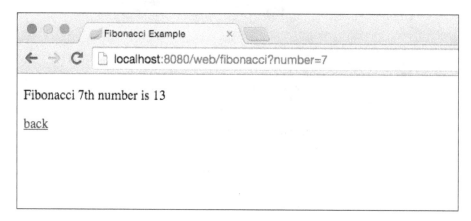

But when we turn off the feature using the following code:

```
features:
    fibonacci:
        restEnabled: true
        webEnabled: false
```

Relaunching the application, we browse to the home page and see that those links are not shown anymore, but we can still access the page if we already know the URL. If we manually write this URL `http://localhost:8080/web/fibonacci?number=15`, we can still access the page with the response.

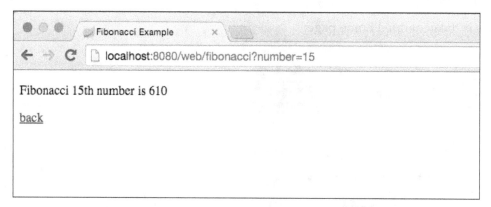

This practice is very useful, but it usually adds unnecessary complexity to your code. Don't forget to refactor the code, deleting old toggles that you won't use anymore. It will keep your code clean and readable. Also, a good point is getting this working without restarting the application. There are many storage options that do not require a restart, databases being the most popular.

Summary

Feature Toggle is a nice way to hide and/or handle partially finished functionalities in production environments. This may sound weird for those deploying code to production on demand, but it is quite common to find this situation when practicing Continuous Integration, Delivery, or Deployment.

We have introduced the technique and discussed the pros and cons of using it. We also enumerated some of the typical cases where toggling features can be helpful.

There are many libraries that can help us to implement this technique, providing a lot of capabilities such as using a web interface to handle features, storing preferences in a database, or allowing access to concrete user profiles.

Finally, we have implemented two different approaches by ourselves: a Feature Toggle with a very simple REST API, and using the Feature Toggle in web applications.

10
Putting It All Together

If you always do what you always did, then you will always get what you always got.

- Albert Einstein

We have gone through a lot of theory followed by even more practice. The entire journey was like a speed train and we have hardly had an opportunity to repeat what we learned. There was no time for rest.

The good news is that the time is now. We'll summarize everything we learned and go through TDD best practices. Some of those have already been mentioned, while others will be new.

TDD in a nutshell

Red-green-refactor is the pillar of TDD that wraps it into a short and repeatable cycle. By short, we mean very short. The time dedicated to each phase is often counted in minutes if not seconds. Write a test, see it fail, write just enough amount of implementation code to make the last test pass, run all tests, and pass into the green phase. Once the minimum code is written so that we have safety in the form of passing tests, it is time to refactor the code until it is as good as we're hoping it to be. While in this phase, tests should always pass. Neither new functionalities nor new tests can be introduced while refactoring is in progress. Doing all this in such a short period of time is often scary, or might sound impossible. We hope that, through the practices we did together, your skills have improved as well as your confidence and speed.

While there is a word *test* in TDD, it is not the main benefit nor objective. TDD is first and foremost a concept of a better way to design our code. On top of that, we end up with tests that should be used to continuously check that the application continues working as expected.

The importance of speed was mentioned often. While part of this is accomplished by us being ever more proficient in TDD, another contributor is *test doubles* (mocking, stubbing, spying, and so on). With these, we can remove the need for external dependencies such as databases, filesystems, third-party services, and so on.

What are the other benefits of TDD? Documentation is one of them. Since code itself is the only accurate and always up-to-date representation of the applications we're working on, specifications written using TDD (being code as well) is the first place we should turn to when we need to better understand what some piece of code does.

How about design? You noticed how TDD produces code that is designed better. Rather than defining design in advance, with TDD it tends to emerge as we progress from one specification to another. At the same time, code that is easy to test is well-designed code. Tests force us to apply some of the coding best practices.

We also learned that TDD does not need to be practiced only on small units (methods). It can also be used at a much higher level where the focus is on a feature or a behavior that can span multiple methods, classes, or even applications and systems. One of the forms of TDD practiced at such a high level is **behavior-driven development (BDD)**. Unlike TDD, which is based on the unit tests that are done by developers for developers, BDD can be used by almost everyone in your organization. Since it tackles behaviors and it's written in natural (ubiquitous) language, testers, managers, business representatives, and others can participate in its creation and use it as a reference later on.

We defined legacy code as code without tests. We faced some of the challenges legacy code puts in front of us and learned some of the techniques that can be used to make it testable.

With all this in mind, let's go through the TDD best practices.

Best practices

Coding best practices are a set of informal rules that the software development community has learned over time, which can help improve the quality of software. While each application needs a level of creativity and originality (after all, we're trying to build something new or better), coding practices help us avoid some of the problems others faced before us. If you're just starting with TDD, it is a good idea to apply some (if not all) of the best practices generated by others.

For easier classification of test-driven development best practices, we divided them into four categories:

- Naming conventions
- Processes
- Development practices
- Tools

As you'll see, not all of them are exclusive to TDD. Since a big part of test-driven development consists of writing tests, many of the best practices presented in the following sections apply to testing in general, while others are related to general coding best practices. No matter the origin, all of them are useful when practicing TDD.

Take the advice with a certain dose of skepticism. Being a great programmer is not only about knowing how to code, but also about being able to decide which practice, framework or style best suits the project and the team. Being agile is not about following someone else's rules, but about knowing how to adapt to circumstances and choose the best tools and practices that suit the team and the project.

Naming conventions

Naming conventions help to organize tests better, so that it is easier for developers to find what they're looking for. Another benefit is that many tools expect that those conventions are followed. There are many naming conventions in use, and those presented here are just a drop in the ocean. The logic is that any naming convention is better than none. Most important is that everyone on the team knows what conventions are being used and are comfortable with them. Choosing *more popular* conventions has the advantage that newcomers to the team can get up to speed fast since they can leverage existing knowledge to find their way around.

Separate the implementation from the test code

Benefits: It avoids accidentally packaging tests together with production binaries; many build tools expect tests to be in a certain source directory.

Common practice is to have at least two source directories. Implementation code should be located in `src/main/java` and test code in `src/test/java`. In bigger projects, the number of source directories can increase but the separation between implementation and tests should remain as is.

Build tools such as Gradle and Maven expect source directories separation as well as naming conventions.

You might have noticed that the `build.gradle` files that we used throughout this book did not have explicitly specified what to test nor what classes to use to create a `.jar` file. Gradle assumes that tests are in `src/test/java` and that the implementation code that should be packaged into a jar file is in `src/main/java`.

Place test classes in the same package as implementation

Benefits: Knowing that tests are in the same package as the code helps finding code faster.

As stated in the previous practice, even though packages are the same, classes are in the separate source directories.

All exercises throughout this book followed this convention.

Name test classes in a similar fashion to the classes they test

Benefits: Knowing that tests have a similar name to the classes they are testing helps in finding the classes faster.

One commonly used practice is to name tests the same as the implementation classes, with the suffix `Test`. If, for example, the implementation class is `TickTackToe`, the test class should be `TickTackToeTest`.

However, in all cases, with the exception of those we used throughout the *refactoring exercises*, we prefer the suffix `Spec`. It helps to make a clear distinction that test methods are primarily created as a way to specify what will be developed. Testing is a great subproduct of those specifications.

Use descriptive names for test methods

Benefits: It helps in understanding the objective of tests.

Using method names that describe tests is beneficial when trying to figure out why some tests failed or when the coverage should be increased with more tests. It should be clear what conditions are set before the test, what actions are performed and what is the expected outcome.

There are many different ways to name test methods and our preferred method is to name them using the *Given/When/Then* syntax used in the BDD scenarios. *Given* describes (pre)conditions, *When* describes actions, and *Then* describes the expected outcome. If some test does not have preconditions (usually set using @Before and @BeforeClass annotations), *Given* can be skipped.

Let's take a look at one of the specifications we created for our *TickTackToe* application:

```
@Test
public void whenPlayAndWholeHorizontalLineThenWinner() {
    ticTacToe.play(1, 1); // X
    ticTacToe.play(1, 2); // O
    ticTacToe.play(2, 1); // X
    ticTacToe.play(2, 2); // O
    String actual = ticTacToe.play(3, 1); // X
    assertEquals("X is the winner", actual);
}
```

Just by reading the name of the method, we can understand what it is about. When we play and the whole horizontal line is populated, then we have a winner.

Do not rely only on comments to provide information about the test objective. Comments do not appear when tests are executed from your favorite IDE nor do they appear in reports generated by CI or build tools.

Processes

TDD processes are the core set of practices. Successful implementation of TDD depends on practices described in this section.

Write a test before writing the implementation code

Benefits: It ensures that testable code is written; ensures that every line of code gets tests written for it.

By writing or modifying the test first, the developer is focused on requirements before starting to work on the implementation code. This is the main difference compared to writing tests after the implementation is done. The additional benefit is that with the tests written first, we are avoiding the danger that the tests work as quality checking instead of quality assurance. We're trying to ensure that quality is built in as opposed to checking later whether we met quality objectives.

Only write new code when the test is failing
Benefits: It confirms that the test does not work without the implementation.

If tests are passing without the need to write or modify the implementation code, then either the functionality is already implemented or the test is defective. If new functionality is indeed missing, then the test always passes and is therefore useless. Tests should fail for the expected reason. Even though there are no guarantees that the test is verifying the right thing, with fail first and for the expected reason, confidence that verification is correct should be high.

Rerun all tests every time the implementation code changes
Benefits: It ensures that there is no unexpected side effect caused by code changes.

Every time any part of the implementation code changes, all tests should be run. Ideally, tests are fast to execute and can be run by the developer locally. Once code is submitted to version control, all tests should be run again to ensure that there was no problem due to code merges. This is specially important when more than one developer is working on the code. Continuous integration tools such as Jenkins (`http://jenkins-ci.org/`), Hudson (`http://hudson-ci.org/`), Travis (`https://travis-ci.org/`), and Bamboo (`https://www.atlassian.com/software/bamboo`) should be used to pull the code from the repository, compile it, and run tests.

All tests should pass before a new test is written
Benefits: The focus is maintained on a small unit of work; implementation code is (almost) always in working condition.

It is sometimes tempting to write multiple tests before the actual implementation. In other cases, developers ignore problems detected by existing tests and move towards new features. This should be avoided whenever possible. In most cases, breaking this rule will only introduce technical debt that will need to be paid with interest. One of the goals of TDD is that the implementation code is (almost) always working as expected. Some projects, due to pressures to reach the delivery date or maintain the budget, break this rule and dedicate time to new features, leaving the task of fixing the code associated with failed tests for later. These projects usually end up postponing the inevitable.

Refactor only after all tests are passing
Benefits: This type of refactoring is safe.

If all implementation code that can be affected has tests and they are all passing, it is relatively safe to refactor. In most cases, there is no need for new tests. Small modifications to existing tests should be enough. The expected outcome of refactoring is to have all tests passing both before and after the code is modified.

Development practices

Practices listed in this section are focused on the best way to write tests.

Write the simplest code to pass the test
Benefits: It ensures cleaner and clearer design; avoids unnecessary features.

The idea is that the simpler the implementation, the better and easier it is to maintain the product. The idea adheres to the **keep it simple stupid (KISS)** principle. This states that most systems work best if they are kept simple rather than made complex; therefore, simplicity should be a key goal in design, and unnecessary complexity should be avoided.

Write assertions first, act later
Benefits: This clarifies the purpose of the requirements and tests early.

Once the assertion is written, the purpose of the test is clear and the developer can concentrate on the code that will accomplish that assertion and, later on, on the actual implementation.

Minimize assertions in each test
Benefits: This avoids assertion roulette; allows execution of more asserts.

If multiple assertions are used within one test method, it might be hard to tell which of them caused a test failure. This is especially common when tests are executed as part of the continuous integration process. If the problem cannot be reproduced on a developer's machine (as may be the case if the problem is caused by environmental issues), fixing the problem may be difficult and time consuming.

When one assert fails, execution of that test method stops. If there are other asserts in that method, they will not be run and information that can be used in debugging is lost.

Last but not least, having multiple asserts creates confusion about the objective of the test.

This practice does not mean that there should always be only one assert per test method. If there are other asserts that test the same logical condition or unit of functionality, they can be used within the same method.

Let's go through few examples:

```
@Test

public final void whenOneNumberIsUsedThenReturnValueIsThatSameNumber()
{
    Assert.assertEquals(3, StringCalculator.add("3"));
}


@Test
public final void whenTwoNumbersAreUsedThenReturnValueIsTheirSum() {
    Assert.assertEquals(3+6, StringCalculator.add("3,6"));
}
```

The preceding code contains two specifications that clearly define what the objective of those tests is. By reading the method names and looking at the assert, there should be clarity on what is being tested. Consider the following for example:

```
@Test
public final void
whenNegativeNumbersAreUsedThenRuntimeExceptionIsThrown() {
    RuntimeException exception = null;
    try {
        StringCalculator.add("3,-6,15,-18,46,33");
    } catch (RuntimeException e) {
        exception = e;
    }
    Assert.assertNotNull("Exception was not thrown", exception);
    Assert.assertEquals("Negatives not allowed: [-6, -18]",
            exception.getMessage());
}
```

This specification has more than one assert, but they are testing the same logical unit of functionality. The first assert is confirming that the exception exists, and the second that its message is correct. When multiple asserts are used in one test method, they should all contain messages that explain the failure. This way debugging the failed assert is easier. In the case of one assert per test method, messages are welcome, but not necessary since it should be clear from the method name what the objective of the test is.

```
@Test
public final void whenAddIsUsedThenItWorks() {
    Assert.assertEquals(0, StringCalculator.add(""));
    Assert.assertEquals(3, StringCalculator.add("3"));
    Assert.assertEquals(3+6, StringCalculator.add("3,6"));
    Assert.assertEquals(3+6+15+18+46+33,
            StringCalculator.add("3,6,15,18,46,33"));
    Assert.assertEquals(3+6+15, StringCalculator.add("3,6n15"));
    Assert.assertEquals(3+6+15,
            StringCalculator.add("//;n3;6;15"));
    Assert.assertEquals(3+1000+6,
            StringCalculator.add("3,1000,1001,6,1234"));
}
```

This test has many asserts. It is unclear what the functionality is, and if one of them fails, it is unknown whether the rest would work or not. It might be hard to understand the failure when this test is executed through some of the CI tools.

Do not introduce dependencies between tests

Benefits: The tests work in any order independently, whether all or only a subset is run

Each test should be independent from the others. Developers should be able to execute any individual test, a set of tests, or all of them. Often, due to the test runner's design, there is no guarantee that tests will be executed in any particular order. If there are dependencies between tests, they might easily be broken with the introduction of new ones.

Tests should run fast

Benefits: These tests are used often.

If it takes a lot of time to run tests, developers will stop using them or run only a small subset related to the changes they are making. The benefit of fast tests, besides fostering their usage, is quick feedback. The sooner the problem is detected, the easier it is to fix it. Knowledge about the code that produced the problem is still fresh. If the developer already started working on the next feature while waiting for the completion of the execution of the tests, he might decide to postpone fixing the problem until that new feature is developed. On the other hand, if he drops his current work to fix the bug, time is lost in context switching.

Tests should be so quick that developers can run all of them after each change without getting bored or frustrated.

Use test doubles

Benefits: This reduces code dependency and test execution will be faster.

Mocks are prerequisites for fast execution of tests and ability to concentrate on a single unit of functionality. By mocking dependencies external to the method that is being tested, the developer is able to focus on the task at hand without spending time in setting them up. In the case of bigger teams, those dependencies might not even be developed. Also, the execution of tests without mocks tends to be slow. Good candidates for mocks are databases, other products, services, and so on.

Use set-up and tear-down methods

Benefits: This allows set-up and tear-down code to be executed before and after the class or each method.

In many cases, some code needs to be executed before the test class or before each method in a class. For this purpose, JUnit has `@BeforeClass` and `@Before` annotations that should be used as the setup phase. `@BeforeClass` executes the associated method before the class is loaded (before the first test method is run). `@Before` executes the associated method before each test is run. Both should be used when there are certain preconditions required by tests. The most common example is setting up test data in the (hopefully in-memory) database.

At the opposite end are `@After` and `@AfterClass` annotations, which should be used as the tear-down phase. Their main purpose is to destroy data or a state created during the setup phase or by the tests themselves. As stated in one of the previous practices, each test should be independent from the others. Moreover, no test should be affected by the others. Tear-down phase helps to maintain the system as if no test was previously executed.

Do not use base classes in tests
Benefits: It provides test clarity.

Developers often approach test code in the same way as implementation. One of the common mistakes is to create base classes that are extended by tests. This practice avoids code duplication at the expense of tests clarity. When possible, base classes used for testing should be avoided or limited. Having to navigate from the test class to its parent, parent of the parent, and so on in order to understand the logic behind tests introduces often unnecessary confusion. Clarity in tests should be more important than avoiding code duplication.

Tools

TDD, coding and testing in general, are heavily dependent on other tools and processes. Some of the most important ones are as follows. Each of them is too big a topic to be explored in this book, so they will be described only briefly.

Code coverage and Continuous integration (CI)
Benefits: It gives assurance that everything is tested

Code coverage practice and tools are very valuable in determining that all code, branches, and complexity is tested. Some of the tools are JaCoCo (`http://www.eclemma.org/jacoco/`), Clover (`https://www.atlassian.com/software/clover/overview`), and Cobertura (`http://cobertura.github.io/cobertura/`).

Continuous Integration (CI) tools are a must for all except the most trivial projects. Some of the most used tools are Jenkins (`http://jenkins-ci.org/`), Hudson (`http://hudson-ci.org/`), Travis (`https://travis-ci.org/`), and Bamboo (`https://www.atlassian.com/software/bamboo`).

Use TDD together with BDD
Benefits: Both developer unit tests and functional customer facing tests are covered.

While TDD with unit tests is a great practice, in many cases, it does not provide all the testing that projects need. TDD is fast to develop, helps the design process, and gives confidence through fast feedback. On the other hand, BDD is more suitable for integration and functional testing, provides better process for requirement gathering through narratives, and is a better way of communicating with clients through scenarios. Both should be used, and together they provide a full process that involves all stakeholders and team members. TDD (based on unit tests) and BDD should be driving the development process. Our recommendation is to use TDD for high code coverage and fast feedback, and BDD as automated acceptance tests. While TDD is mostly oriented towards white-box, BDD often aims at black-box testing. Both TDD and BDD are trying to focus on quality assurance instead of quality checking.

This is just the beginning

You might have expected that by the time you reached the end of this book, you'd know everything about test-driven development. If that was the case, we're sorry that we'll have to disappoint you. It takes a lot of time and practice to master any craft, and TDD is no exception. Go on, apply what you have learned to your projects. Share knowledge with your colleagues. Most importantly, practice, practice and practice. As with Karate, only through continuous practice and repetition, can one fully master test-driven development. We have been using it for a long time, and we still often face new challenges and learn new ways to improve our craftsmanship.

This does not have to be the end

Writing this book was a long journey filled with many adventures. We hope you enjoyed reading it as much as we enjoyed writing it.

We share our experience on a wide variety of subjects at our blog `http://technologyconversations.com`.

Index

H

Hamcrest
about 27, 28
defining 27
URL 28
Hudson
URL 246

I

IDEA demo project 20, 21
implementation, Connect4
requisites 110-118
URL 118
Integrated development environment 20
integration tests
about 80, 159-162
defining 158
test, separating 158, 159
IntelliJ IDEA
Gradle/Java project, setting up 48-51

J

JaCoCo
about 30
URL 30, 251
Java build tools
references 19
JBehave
about 174
final validation 186, 187
JBehave runner 174, 175
PhantomJS browser, installing 179-185
running, with Gradle 176, 177
Selenide 178
Selenium 178
URL 171
Jenkins
URL 246
Jongo 32
JUnit
about 22-25
environment, setting up 48
references 25
URL 23

JUnit assert
comparing, with Hamcrest assert 28

K

Kata exercise
about 201
black-box testing 202
description 201
extract and override call technique 213, 214
legacy code algorithm, applying 207
legacy Kata 201
new feature, adding 202
preliminary investigation 204-206
primitive obsession, removing with
status as Int 218-221
spike testing 202
technical comments 202
keep it simple stupid (KISS)
about 107, 247
URL 107

L

legacy code
defining 190
example 190-193
lack, of dependency injection 195
legacy code change algorithm 196
recognizing 194, 195
legacy code algorithm
about 207
BookRepository dependency, injecting 213
end-to-end test cases, writing 207-210
test cases, automating 210-213
legacy code change algorithm
about 196
applying 196-200
break dependencies 198-200
change points, identifying 196
test points, finding 197, 198
tests, writing 200
legacyutils
URL 198

M

Maven Central
  URL 19
methods, Mockito
  mock() 137
  spy() 137
  verify() 137
Minimum Viable Product (MVP) 168
mocking 8, 134
Mockito
  about 34, 35
  defining 137
  URL 35
mock objects
  defining 136, 137
mocks
  using 134, 135
MongoDB
  URL 31
MongoDB driver 32

N

narrative, BDD
  goals 168

O

Occam's razor
  about 107
  URL 107

P

Parameterize Constructor technique
  URL 199
partial mocking 144
pattern
  URL 199
PhantomJS browser
  URL 179
ping pong game
  defining 5
Postman
  about 207
  URL 207

preliminary investigation
  candidates, finding for refactoring 205
  new feature, defining 206
primitive obsession
  URL 218
Product Owner (PO) 202, 206

Q

quality assurance (QA) 7
quality checking (QC) 7
query
  URL 231

R

README, in markdown format
  URL 166
red-green-refactor process
  about 51
  all tests, running 52
  implementation code, writing 52
  refactoring 53
  repeat 53
  test, writing 51, 52
remote controlled ship
  developing 85
  helper classes 88
  project, setting up 86
  requirements 85-103
RestAssured
  URL 212
REST service 227
Rule
  about 55
  URL 55

S

Selenide
  URL 178
Selenium
  URL 178
setup method
  using 142
Single Responsibility Principle
  about 131
  references 131

Thank you for buying
Test-Driven Java Development

About Packt Publishing

Packt, pronounced 'packed', published its first book, *Mastering phpMyAdmin for Effective MySQL Management*, in April 2004, and subsequently continued to specialize in publishing highly focused books on specific technologies and solutions.

Our books and publications share the experiences of your fellow IT professionals in adapting and customizing today's systems, applications, and frameworks. Our solution-based books give you the knowledge and power to customize the software and technologies you're using to get the job done. Packt books are more specific and less general than the IT books you have seen in the past. Our unique business model allows us to bring you more focused information, giving you more of what you need to know, and less of what you don't.

Packt is a modern yet unique publishing company that focuses on producing quality, cutting-edge books for communities of developers, administrators, and newbies alike. For more information, please visit our website at www.packtpub.com.

About Packt Open Source

In 2010, Packt launched two new brands, Packt Open Source and Packt Enterprise, in order to continue its focus on specialization. This book is part of the Packt Open Source brand, home to books published on software built around open source licenses, and offering information to anybody from advanced developers to budding web designers. The Open Source brand also runs Packt's Open Source Royalty Scheme, by which Packt gives a royalty to each open source project about whose software a book is sold.

Writing for Packt

We welcome all inquiries from people who are interested in authoring. Book proposals should be sent to author@packtpub.com. If your book idea is still at an early stage and you would like to discuss it first before writing a formal book proposal, then please contact us; one of our commissioning editors will get in touch with you.

We're not just looking for published authors; if you have strong technical skills but no writing experience, our experienced editors can help you develop a writing career, or simply get some additional reward for your expertise.

Test-Driven Python Development

ISBN: 978-1-78398-792-4   Paperback: 264 pages

Develop high-quality and maintainable
Python applications using the principles of
test-driven development

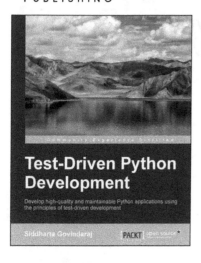

1. Write robust and easily maintainable code
   using the principles of test driven development.

2. Get solutions to real-world problems faced
   by Python developers.

3. Go from a unit testing beginner to a master
   through a series of step-by-step tutorials that
   are easy to follow.

Scala for Java Developers

ISBN: 978-1-78328-363-7   Paperback: 282 pages

Build reactive, scalable applications and integrate
Java code with the power of Scala

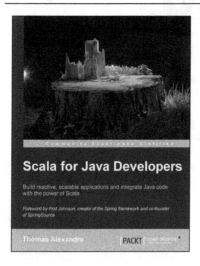

1. Learn the syntax interactively to smoothly
   transition to Scala by reusing your Java code.

2. Leverage the full power of modern web
   programming by building scalable and
   reactive applications.

3. Easy to follow instructions and real world
   examples to help you integrate java code
   and tackle big data challenges.

Please check **www.PacktPub.com** for information on our titles

open source*
community experience distilled

[PACKT]
PUBLISHING

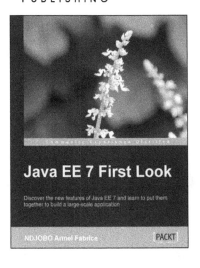

Java EE 7 First Look

ISBN: 978-1-84969-923-5   Paperback: 188 pages

Discover the new features of Java EE 7 and learn to put them together to build a large-scale application

1. Explore changes brought in by the Java EE 7 platform.

2. Master the new specifications that have been added in Java EE to develop applications without any hassle.

3. Quick guide on the new features introduced in Java EE7.

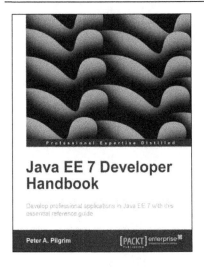

Java EE 7 Developer Handbook

ISBN: 978-1-84968-794-2   Paperback: 634 pages

Develop professional applicaitons in Java EE 7 with this essential reference guide

1. Learn about integration test development on Java EE with Arquillian Framework and the Gradle build system.

2. Learn about containerless builds featuring the GlassFish 4.0 embedded application server.

3. Master Java EE 7 with this example-based, up-to-date guide with descriptions and explanations.

Please check **www.PacktPub.com** for information on our titles